CONTENTS

Acknowledgments

The publisher acknowledges with appreciation permission to use copyrighted material from the following sources:

Harper & Row, Publishers, for quotations from *The Pupil and the Teacher* by Luther A. Weigle, *Realistic Theology* by Walter Marshall Horton, and *The Kingdom of God in America* by H. Richard Niebuhr.

Houghton Mifflin Company for quotations from *Progressive Religious Thought in America: A Survey of the Enlarging Pilgrim Faith* by John Wright Buckham.

The Macmillan Company for quotations from *Can Religious Education Be Christian?* by Harrison S. Elliott.

National Council of the Churches of Christ in the U.S.A. for a quotation from *Christian Education Today: A Statement of Basic Philosophy.* Approved February, 1940, by the Educational Commission (Chicago: The International Council of Religious Education, 1940).

Charles Scribner's Sons for quotations from *God in Christ: Three Discourses Delivered at New Haven, Cambridge, and Andover, with a Preliminary Dissertation on Language* by Horace Bushnell.

Yale University Press for quotations from *Children and Puritanism: The Place of Children in the Life and Thought of the New England Churches, 1620–1847* by Sandford Fleming.

BUSHNELL REDISCOVERED

BUSHNELL REDISCOVERED

William R. Adamson

UNITED CHURCH PRESS
philadelphia · boston

INTRODUCTION

Horace Bushnell has been called the "father" of the Christian education movement in America.[1] He was a genius, a sensitive and much loved pastor, a man of profound insights and controversial ideas, and one of the great historical figures in the life of the Christian church in America. In recent years scholars have led in the rediscovery of his thought and its implications. For those who are unacquainted with the richness of his contributions, Bushnell proves a rewarding source of inspiration and amazement. Many are the writers who have paid tribute to the unique contribution he made to the Christian education of children,[2] for his writings set forth with extraordinary clarity the educational ministry of the Christian church. Indeed, American theologians have been struggling ever since to reconcile the educational ministry with the evangelistic ministry in the long controversy precipitated by Bushnell.[3]

Fresh insights have been gained in the realm of theology from Bushnell's day to the present. The relationship of man with his God is so profound that mankind continues to achieve new perceptions of truth concerning the nature of God and his will for men. Perhaps it would be more accurate to say that gradually men are enabled to perceive more deeply the revelation that God offers. In addition, the social and cultural patterns in the world today are changing with startling rapidity. A living theology must be continually reinterpreted to speak meaningfully to people caught up in such a transition. Conversely, men must be increasingly sensitive to perceive the new revelations of truth that God would give to them within the complexities and dynamic changes of modern life.

The whole movement of Christian education today is involved in this social transition and reinterpretation of theology. When new theologies are brought forth, the premises and philosophies of Christian education must be reexamined and improved. Gone are the days of depending on gimmicks. Modern Christians are asking, "What theology can support both the educational and the evangelistic phases of the ministry of the Christian gospel?" To answer this question, new depth and relevance are required in the interrelationship of the theology and the method employed in the educational task of the church.

Because of this deep struggle going on within Christian education today, because of the new demand for theology and the relentless search for a relevant one, because of the attempt to correlate a dynamic theology with sound educational practice—because of all this, Horace Bushnell and other trailblazing thinkers are coming into new prominence.

Since Bushnell was the one who introduced into the church in America a new emphasis on the educational phase of the Christian ministry to children, contributing one of the two poles of thought in the controversy that expanded within Christian education, a wider understanding of his basic principles carries with it a high priority. This is especially so since his major thesis has been the guiding light of all modern religious education.[4]

Have his theories made as profound an impact as suggested by the claim that he was the father of the Christian education movement in America? Has he truly been a pioneer in this vast movement? What are the insights and ideas that make him so important in the field of Christian education? What are the strengths and weaknesses of his ideas? How did he influence the life of the church in America? These are some of the questions that are receiving new attention today as a part of the rediscovery of Horace Bushnell.

Primarily a preacher, Bushnell spent twenty-six years in the pastorate at Hartford, Connecticut, where he was close to his people and sensitive to the various currents of thought in pioneer America. His was a practical concern for the interpretation of the Christian gospel to his people, for the wholesome application of religion to everyday life. As he struggled to correct some of the unfortunate attitudes and practices within the church of his day, he made many proposals and suggestions that were to have long-range implications for both theology and Christian education. Of the many published sermons, articles, lectures, and theological books that he wrote, his book on Christian education entitled *Christian Nurture* has proved to be his classic work.[5]

From the very beginning, his original articles stirred up strong and heated controversies. The criticism of the theology underlying Bushnell's *Christian Nurture* continues in the present time. Many of his reviewers devote most of their space and effort to tracing the historical sequence of events which led him into these disputes, neglecting to give proper value to his important practical ideas on Christian education.

It is also true that Bushnell has often been misinterpreted. He turned out a great volume of writing, which appeared over a century ago and seems dated and dry to us today. Reading Bushnell thoroughly is therefore a formidable task. Nevertheless, in his works are rare gems of insight that are startlingly modern and that make the study of his works rewarding.

His style is unique. He was not a precise thinker; he used many pictorial illustrations and analogies to suggest meanings that he felt words in themselves could never precisely convey. Hence his style contrasts with the forms of expressions used by most of his colleagues, and this produced much misunderstanding.

As a result of the great doctrinal elaborations and fierce religious debates in New England, Bushnell found that many of the theological words current then had such emotional overtones and such variety of connotation that he was forced to use comparisons and terms from everyday life to suggest the shade

of meaning he wanted to convey.[6] As a result he was continually under suspicion of a "naturalism" that was not deemed
compatible with the Christian gospel. This factor continues to
color some of the criticism of him by modern writers.

There is an urgent need today to give a clear and fair exposition of Bushnell's educational ideas, to see his writings in
context, and to let him speak for himself. Bushnell is remembered primarily as the author of *Christian Nurture*, or as the
originator of a few choice sentences, but aside from this the
knowledge of what he said and wrote is far too meager.

His practical ideas and methods should be of immediate
interest to present-day parents and teachers. These nuggets of
truth might well have come from a twentieth-century educational text; their relationship to the modern scene needs to be
kept continually in mind. The difficult circumstances and the
unhappy situations within the church that prompted Bushnell
to bring forth his innovations also merit examination.

Horace Bushnell was acutely aware of the interrelationship
between theology and Christian education. He knew that
Christian education without a strong and dynamic theology
lacks direction and power, and that conversely, Christian theology without a dynamic educational outreach suitable to the
contemporary scene soon becomes sterile and obsolete. Part of
the greatness of his lasting contribution can be seen in his surprising integration of educational practice with theology.

This book, consisting of four parts, attempts to view the
contributions of Bushnell from a new perspective.

The first part is entitled "Pioneer Educator." Here is given
an exposition of his practical ideas of Christian nurture. His
remarks, directed primarily to parents rather than to educational experts, reveal his keen sensitivity and understanding of
human nature. He proclaimed truths a hundred years ahead
of his time—truths that are now corroborated by scientific investigation.

He sought to interpret to the people of his time the nature
of the mysterious and redemptive relationship of a person with
his God. This effort produced, as by-products, many worthy

and lasting suggestions for church school leaders and for parents who are training children in the Christian way of life.

The second part consists of an exposition of Bushnell as a "Champion of Children." It gives the background of the situations in which he found himself. It includes a brief outline of some of the developments in doctrine and practice within the Calvinism found in the Congregational churches of New England. Because there is so much emphasis on Christian nurture in churches today, it is difficult to grasp the unfortunate situation with which Bushnell was wrestling.

He cut through the confusion of New England theology, struggled with the dilemma of the period, and came up with a theory that restored children to a new dignity and status within the church. He consistently maintained a distinction between childhood and adulthood, emphasizing the need for continuous decisions all through a Christian's life.

The third part of the book deals with Bushnell as a "Provocative Theologian." It is a summary treatment of the main points of his theology, which forms the basis of his educational classic, *Christian Nurture*. The various strands of his thinking are drawn together into chapters that show how many points of his theology relate to his educational theory.

The final part shows how Bushnell's doctrine of nurture fits into the historical development of the thought patterns of America both in theology and in the great expansion of Christian educational work in the churches. In conclusion, a critical evaluation is offered of his enduring significance in relation to the past and the future.

PART I   PIONEER EDUCATOR

chapter 1 THE MAN
             BEHIND
             THE IDEA

Horace Bushnell was a genius. He was a brilliant, transitional figure who introduced a new era in American religious thought. Before proceeding to look at his ideas, before considering his dominant theme of Christian nurture, it is important to look at least briefly at the man himself. Several exhaustive biographies and many short treatments of his life have already been written.[1] All that is necessary here is an outline of Bushnell's distinguishing characteristics which seem to have special significance for his achievements in the realm of Christian education.

INTUITIVE AND CREATIVE

Bushnell was a thoroughly unique personality. Everyone who came in contact with him immediately sensed this. Apparently he became conscious of his peculiar powers and realized even in his youth that he was different, that he was a leader and would have to strike out on his own.[2] He had a most creative imagination, with a powerful gift of intuitive insight that bordered on the mystical.

His religious insights became increasingly experiential and were climaxed in 1848 with a powerful "revelation" or "illumination" from God. At this time he perceived in a new fashion the truths and glory of God. His daughter relates how he came

13

from his study after several hours of writing with his eyes shining and his hair fairly standing on end, as if from electricity.[3]

In striking contrast to the theologians of his time with their clanking, mechanical logic and their persistent elaboration of religious dogma and formulas, Bushnell arrived with his ability to "see" truth. Just as a playwright often "hears" what he will write in his moment of inspiration, so Bushnell was able to see truth. The new insights would suddenly appear with clarity and power. He has even been called a "seer."

In addition, he expressed himself in words of eloquence and beauty. He might, with equal justification, be described as a poet-teacher or a poet-theologian. He himself once said, "Poets, then, are the true metaphysicians." [4]

An original thinker who saw things from a different angle and interpreted them in his own way, he could never be a follower of others; but at the same time he was not the type of leader who could serve as a model for a school of followers. According to his contemporaries, his ideal was more that of discovery than of painstaking research. He had little patience with large libraries and the working over of old ideas. He wanted to be out on the frontier pushing across new horizons of thought. While this was his strength, there were times when such a tendency proved a real weakness. There was validity in the criticism that he published first and read later. One contemporary said of him:

> Perhaps if he had been more of a plodder, and had taken time to make himself familiar with other men's thoughts, he might have saved himself some trouble. But it was easier for him to create than to absorb; he was a composer and not a reader, a fountain and not a cistern.[5]

ROOTED IN LAW

Bushnell was a trained lawyer. He had almost completed his law training at Yale College when he decided to go into the ministry. His earlier training was an important factor in his

14

life, one that was manifested throughout his work. His father
had been a justice of the peace in the local district where they
lived and had often asked his youthful son to give his judgment upon cases that the father had to decide. This served
to give him an early taste of law as well as a concern for justice
and righteousness. Moreover, the church influence of his youth
was a logical and legalistic Calvinism, the sort of thing that
thoroughly impregnated his youthful character.[6]

The law training strongly influenced his sharp mind that
already had a flair for discourse. His fellow students in college
attested to the relish with which he entered into debate, the
force and skill he displayed. When he tackled a problem or
a controversial issue, it soon became obvious that he was out
"to win his case."

In his first few published articles he displayed an ability
for scorching thrusts and sarcasm toward the persons with whom
he was in disagreement. Here was the lawyer using every subtle
and devastating tool of debate to discredit and to overcome the
opponent. Bushnell regretted these incidents in later years,
finding that such tactics did not suit his new calling.

It was characteristic that his writings were often "relentless" and "massive" in their treatment of a subject. His attention to details of explanation, clarification, and illustration resulted in a great volume of argumentation. A more precise
ability to go to the heart of an issue and to state it in succinct
terms would have secured a wider reading of his works in modern times. In contrast to his theological treatises, his shorter
sermons and his *Christian Nurture* reveal this more appealing
lucidity.

PARADOX

Another important factor must be noted. There was a certain
paradox within the life of Bushnell from which he never really
freed himself. By nature he was intuitive, possessed of a very
creative imagination. The greatness of his religious life was
due in part to the experiential application of such imagination.
He saw that the Christian faith involved a personal, direct re-

15

lationship with God as he is known through Jesus Christ. He realized the personal and moral nature of this relationship with a loving, personal God. This was the high point of his contribution to theology. It was in stark contrast to the prevailing emphasis on a rather arbitrary, sovereign God who could elect men to damnation if he chose, and whose motives and choices were not to be questioned by men.

Yet in his treatises Bushnell was continuously switching back to considerations of law and to legalistic elements. This tendency proved a hindrance and sometimes obscured the genius and value of his new religious insights. It must be said, though, that Bushnell's emphasis on righteousness and character saved him from the perils of mysticism.

But he could never quite separate himself from the influence of his youthful environment in spite of his far-reaching insights. Even in his last work, *Forgiveness and Law*, he was wrestling with this paradox; he was struggling to reconcile these two elements.[7] When Bushnell reached the apogee of his insights, he made a valuable contribution to American theology. However, at the opposite end of his orbit, the force of gravity issuing from the matter of law, in which he was trained and by which he was continually intrigued, brought him close to earth and sometimes threatened him with destruction.

A MAN'S MAN

Horace Bushnell was a man's man. He was robust and powerful in physique and striking in appearance. He was reared on a New England farm where the hardy features of that life were impressed upon him. His enthusiasm for work was boundless, whether it involved heavy manual labor on the farm or the mechanical skills needed to operate his father's little factory for the processing of homespun cloth. He boasted of his ability to put in a fourteen-hour workday during his teens and of his interest and skill in stonemasonry.

A revealing incident from his school days shows his spirit. He was a good-natured boy, inclined to be rather quiet and shy, but he did not let this quality become a disadvantage:

16

Awaking suddenly to the perception of the fact that his good nature was mistaken for weakness, and that he was being made the butt of the school bullies, he chose the roughest and the most intolerable of these, a much bigger boy than himself, and gave him, in the presence of the school, so spirited a thrashing as to establish his own character for courage beyond a doubt. No more fighting was necessary, and he was glad to relapse into his old peaceable relations with his schoolmates.[8]

As a teenager of sixteen and seventeen he enjoyed wrestling and challenged some of the best wrestlers in the region. Everything he did was characterized by great vigor. All of his life he had a passion for fishing. From youth to old age he enjoyed hiking off to remote streams and lakes to engage in his favorite sport. The rural atmosphere of his youth and those frequent expeditions into the wilds brought to his sensitive spirit a keen appreciation of the beauties of nature.

Unfortunately as early as 1839, when he was thirty-seven, a throat ailment began. This was followed by a chronic cough and a lung condition, which gradually increased its grip upon him. Yet he fought on doggedly, working until his strength was gone, then going away for a rest and again returning to his work.

On a trip to Europe for his health, he walked as much as eighteen miles a day over steep mountain roads in the Alps. On a trip to California for health purposes, he traveled up and down the countryside surveying land levels and gathering data for potential sites upon which to establish a university. When his disease was at an advanced stage and overexertion caused him to expectorate mouthfuls of blood, he insisted on guiding some companions over unchartered, rough countryside to show them the feasibility of a new route that he had conceived.

INDIVIDUALISM

His individualism was another characteristic prominent throughout his life. At the age of sixteen, when he was attending the Classical School on New Preston Hill, he refused to take his

17

turn as a monitor. He declared that he had come there to study and not to watch over other students. At Yale College he would never enter into recitation contests for distinction. He found elocution exercises so unreal and awkward that he would often forget his lines and sit down in the middle of his address. Yet when there was a true issue he could speak with ease. His independence was painfully obvious in the Divinity School at New Haven, for he never fully agreed with what he believed to be the mechanical method of thought used there.

This sort of individualism helped him to introduce his revolution into the life of the church. It helped him to stand his ground when he became the center of much controversy and the target of much hostility. Published reviews were caustic; repeated attempts to hold a heresy trial were made; neighboring pulpits were closed against him. Yet he knew that many of his insights were true and would ultimately prevail. Before the publication of some of his important works, his letters to his wife and friends indicate that he knew the sort of outburst that would result. He went ahead deliberately.

SPIRITUAL GROWTH

Horace Bushnell was the product of a fine type of Christian nurture and, therefore, he could speak of it authentically as a pastor. Both his father and mother were persons of wholesome character. His father was a Methodist, his mother an Episcopalian; they attended the only church nearby, which was Congregational.

At the age of seventeen, while tending his father's carding machinery, he wrote a paper of true insight touching on religious doctrines—election, predestination, the sovereignty of God, and such topics as he would hear discussed in church. When he was almost nineteen, he committed himself to his Lord and Savior and subsequently joined the church.

At Yale he gave himself fully to an intellectual emphasis and soon found himself so full of doubts that his religious faith faded. Yet his character and moral standing did not in any way degenerate after the fashion of many of his colleagues. Fol-

18

lowing graduation and a period of schoolteaching to pay off his debts, after an editorship and a half-year of law training, he decided to enter the practice of law in Ohio. This decision was made in spite of an offer to assume a tutorship of law at Yale. At this point his mother exerted some diplomatic and well-timed influence so that he was persuaded to return to Yale. Near the end of his law training he decided to go into the Christian ministry.

In the winter of 1831 a revival swept Yale. Practically everyone was touched by it except Bushnell and his class. By now he was a successful and popular tutor and his class imitated his example of resistance. Apparently, because of his sense of duty and his feeling of responsibility for his students, his conscience led him to make a new decision for Christ. It was essentially a simple and profound desire to be and do right, rather than to have a personal relationship with God. He found that the moral obligation of doing right and serving God to the best of his knowledge was of paramount importance, and that intellectual doubts were less important and could be deferred. Though it was a unique kind of conversion, it was, nevertheless, a complete "turning about" and he was a changed man. In a few months he had left law for the ministry.

In February of 1833 he was called to North Congregational Church in Hartford, Connecticut. He was ordained in May and was married to Mary Apthorp of New Haven in September. So began his labors in the ministry and the experience of family life. Of the five children born into the family, an infant daughter died in 1837. His mother died in 1838. Then in 1842 his only son died at the age of four. His thoughts were thus pushed into a deep consideration of the future life and from his lips came the poignant statement, "I have learned more of experimental religion since my little boy died than in all my life before." [9]

His greatest religious experience came in 1848. The ceaseless activity of his mind during almost fifteen years of serving his people coupled with his personal sorrows brought him ever closer to a new relationship with God.

At that time he had been reading various devotional and spiritual classics. On a February morning it was evident that something unusual had happened. His wife asked him, "What have you seen?" He replied, "The gospel." He had had a revelation from the mind of God himself. He was now able to enter into a closer relationship with God—a personal friendship, as it were. Referring to his experience he said, "I was set on by the personal discovery of Christ, and of God as represented in him." [10]

This new illumination immediately moved him to write his famous sermon "Christ, the Form of the Soul." [11] It gave him a fresh and powerful impetus to produce the many writings that continued to the end of his life. Following this high peak in his spiritual life he said:

> Christian faith is the faith of a transaction. It is not the committing of one's thought in assent to any proposition, but the trusting of one's being to *a being*, there to be rested, kept, guided, molded, governed, and possessed forever. . . . It gives you God, fills you with God in immediate, experimental knowledge, puts you in possession of all there is in him, and allows you to be invested with his character itself. [12]

A GROWING MIND

It is important to note the operation of Bushnell's mind. He had the faculty of letting ideas grow gradually and steadily without forcing them. This probably stemmed, in part, from his discovery in the Yale revival that intellectual doubts were not the whole issue and did not all have to be solved at once. He states the procedure that he followed in these words:

> Never be in a hurry to believe; never try to conquer doubts against time. . . . One of the greatest talents in religious discovery is the finding how to hang up questions and let them hang without being at all anxious about them. Turn a free glance at them now

and then as they hang; move freely about them, and see
them first on one side and then on another, and by-
and-by, when you turn some corner of thought, you will
be delighted and astonished to see how quietly and easily they open their secret and let you in! [13]

Bushnell seems to have had many of these "questions," as
well as other germinal ideas, in his fertile mind even from
youthful days. He was busy developing these throughout his
whole life. This gives a certain unity and coherence to his
writings; this makes it important to interpret him in light of his
whole message and thought.

While in Divinity School in 1832, he wrote an essay comparing the methods of natural and moral philosophy, showing
that the method of the former could not be applied to the latter. Here he began to question the logic and philosophy prevalent in his time. Here was the beginning of one of his major works, *Nature and the Supernatural*, which he completed in
1858, some thirty years later.[14] In the same year (1832) he
wrote another essay attempting to prove the existence of a Moral
Governor in the universe from the ingenious use of his own
theory of the origin of language. This study on language he
perfected fifteen years later, incorporating it into *God in Christ*,
one of his most famous books.

His theory of language became central to everything he
wrote. These facts reveal the trend of his thoughts from 1847,
when he published his *Discourses on Christian Nurture*,[15] to
1861, when he published the final and extended volume of
Christian Nurture.[16] Actually his ideas on nurture began to appear in germinal form in periodical articles as early as 1838.[17]
An earlier sermon on "Christian Forgiveness" eventually gave
rise to the two volumes of *Vicarious Sacrifice*, the first volume
being published in 1866 and the second volume in 1874.[18]
These were his last works and very dear to him. The task of
finishing this treatment on the large subject of atonement drove
him on and helped him to maintain life in a wasted body during his last few years.

21

Bushnell lived in an exciting and eventful period in American history. For instance, he came in contact with the Vigilantes during his trip to California in 1856. He knew men like Edward Beecher, Charles Finney, and Washington Gladden. He carefully followed the events and politics of the American Civil War and used some of those tragic incidents in his sermons and lectures. The new movement of biblical criticism and a more scientific study of the Bible was presenting a serious new challenge. Darwin had written his *Origin of Species* in 1859, but because of the war it had not come immediately to the attention of the American public. During his last years Bushnell began to grapple with the writings of Darwin and Spencer.

Horace Bushnell was a man of many interests and abilities as a naturalist, surveyor, road engineer, housebuilder, mechanic, park designer, traveler, fisherman, and preacher. His character and versatility distinguished him from other men of his day. It was this man of many talents who in the final analysis pushed open new frontiers in the field of Christian education and made his major contribution there.

chapter 2 INSIGHTS CONCERNING THE VERY YOUNG

Bushnell had the happy faculty of being able to observe people and families, and then to gauge with remarkable accuracy their innermost conflicts. In his pastoral visitations he had ample opportunity for such observation and evaluation. Time and again his descriptions of family life in *Christian Nurture* reveal his ability to make a penetrating analysis of what was really going on within the homes of the parishioners he visited. As he struggled with his pastoral work, as he encountered the unfortunate results of the current revivalism, as he began to formulate the alternate method of nurture for children, he became increasingly observant of what took place between parents and children. His own experience as a father sharpened his perception of the growth of children.

Gradually through his experience, observation, and reading, he shaped and confirmed his convictions about the proper nurture of children. His statements made in the context of his time were of such authenticity that he formulated the beginnings of a true child psychology for the American people. His ideas have a startling affinity with those of modern textbooks in psychology and education.[1] The general principles he proposed in his century accurately marked the direction that the scientific investigation of the twentieth century would take.

DEVELOPMENTAL STAGES

Bushnell achieved a clear understanding of the developmental stages of childhood. This was an insight of far-reaching significance. In present-day child psychology the understanding of the various stages of growth with their characteristic abilities, needs, and learning tasks is a basic concern affecting most all educational endeavors. Today it has become a much-investigated and highly detailed study.[2] While Bushnell did not have the terminology of the "developmental stages," he did have the essential knowledge of it.

This was a singular achievement in his day when the adult phases of religion were forced upon children. Although a new understanding of the child was coming into prominence, Bushnell was one of the first to incorporate it thoroughly into religious life.

Bushnell had his own way of distinguishing the two main stages of childhood:

> It is the distinction between the age of *impressions* and the age of *tuitional influences*; or between the *age of existence in the will of the parent*, and the age of *will and personal choice in the child*. If the distinction were laid between the age previous to language and the age of language, it would amount to nearly the same thing.[3]

Thus, for his lines of demarcation, he relies upon the change from the purely emotional to the increasing intellectual capacities of the child, upon language ability, and upon what currently would be called the "development of the ego-concept." [4] Hence, Bushnell not only had a good grasp of the growth process in childhood but also made a notable attempt at fitting Christian teaching to the capacities of the child at each stage.

24

THE NATURE OF INFANCY

Bushnell spoke with fervor about the "stage of impressions." Though he did not possess today's terminology or detailed knowledge concerning the subconscious mind, he still perceived the significance of impressions upon the emotional or subconscious strata of the child's mind.

He demonstrated the powerful influence of the parents on the infant and pointed out that the infant, who is not a complete individual, has many potential powers. All the time he is being influenced and molded not by intellectual things but by "impressions." He speaks of the baby as a "passive lump," but he also knows that it is a very receptive and sensitive lump. He could see the profound influence that parents and family have upon a developing personality, although he did recognize that there will be individual characteristics and that outside influences will have a partial influence on every person.

THE CARE OF INFANTS

Bushnell stated that more is done for the shaping of the child's character in the first three years of life than in all the training and teaching that follows. This indeed was a most startling statement in his day. He had an extraordinary understanding of the infant period. The small child "opens into conscious life under the soul of the parent, streaming into his eyes and ears, through the *manners* and *tones* of the nursery." [5] It is soon to be observed that:

> A smile wakens a smile; any kind of sentiment or passion, playing in the face of the parent, wakens a responsive sentiment or passion. Irritation irritates, a frown withers, love expands a look congenial to itself, and why not holy love? [6]

Though the infant cannot comprehend words, Bushnell knows how the feeling tones are communicated in the very care of the child. He writes:

25

Who is ignorant that by jerks of passion, flashes of irritation, unsteady changes of caprice and nervousness, fits of self-indulgence, disgusts with self and life that are half the time allowed to include the child, songs and caresses both of day and night, that are volunteered as much to compose the mother's or the nurse's impatience as the child's—who is ignorant that an infant, *handled in this manner*, may be kept in a continual fret of torment and ill-nature.[7]

Just at the time when such crucial things are taking place, just when they have a golden opportunity to shape the future character and destiny of the child, lamented Bushnell, many parents, failing to see their responsibilities, put their child into the hands of a nurse or attendant. Even if the nurse be well chosen, would not the mother be dismayed at the thought of the child's growing into the likeness of the nurse instead of herself? Concerning this practice, Bushnell observed:

Such a mother ought to see that she is making much more of herself than of her child. This whole scheme of nurture is a scheme of self-indulgence. Now is the time when her little one most needs to see her face, and hear her voice, and feel her gentle hand. Now is the time when her child's eternity pleads most entreatingly for the benefit of her motherly charge and presence.[8]

IMPRESSIONS AND MEANINGS

The child receives his first lessons from the looks and faces round about him. And what he sees is important. The child should be surrounded with an atmosphere of security and happiness during his early years.

Bushnell anticipated the question that would probably be asked by parents of his day. What kind of religious training can be given a young child before he can talk, before he can be told about God and Christ and religious matters? Everything that the child sees, hears, and feels is building attitudes and forming deep impressions. So Bushnell explains:

26

Observe, again, how very quick the child's eye is, in the passive age of infancy, to catch impressions and *receive the meaning* of looks, voices, and motions. It peruses all faces and colors and sounds. Every sentiment that looks into its eyes, looks back out of its eyes, and plays in miniature on its countenance. The tear that steals down the cheek of a mother's suppressed grief, gathers the little infantile face into a responsive sob. With a kind of wondering silence, which is the next thing to adoration, it studies the mother in her prayer, and looks up piously with her, in that exploring watch that signifies unspoken prayer.[9]

Then he makes a profound statement, which has far-reaching implications. He says that language itself has no meaning until rudimentary impressions and meanings have been established in experience.

According to Bushnell, the word light does not signify anything until the eye has experienced light. Even more significantly—especially for child psychology and education—the word love is meaningless to the child who has not received love, and the word God is meaningless until some previous idea of such a reality has been generated. Bushnell was quite aware of the important process going on within the child before the power of language begins—or, again, in order that the power of language might begin. He would impress upon parents the great care and wisdom needed, for here are the roots of religion.[10]

Surprisingly, Bushnell observed even in his day the subtle but devastating impact of rejection upon the infant's mind. He speaks vividly of the parents who secretly do not want or will not accept the newborn child:

It may be [that] the mother especially does not accept the child willingly, but only submits to the maternal office and charge, as to some hard necessity. This charge is going to detain her at home, and limit her freedom. Or it will take her away from the shows and pleasures for which she is living. Or it will burden her

27

days and nights with cares that weary her self-indulgence. Or she is not fond of children, and never means
to be fond of them—they are not worth the trouble
they cost.[11]

"Fatal mischief" is his term for that which results from this
cruel denial of affection, from this underlying attitude which
neighbors and friends may never see or suspect, but which the
child perceives all too well.

"Anything which puts the child aloof from the parent, or
takes away the confidence of love and sympathy, will as certainly be a wall to shut him away from God."[12] Parents may
resort to abuse and harsh words as punishment that wounds the
child's tender feelings. Very often it has been the impatience,
irritability, arbitrariness, or inept management of the parent
that disturbed and upset the child in the first place.

If the child's relationships with other children in school or
at play are continuously surrounded by parental fear that he
may get hurt, or do something wrong, the child may become
crippled psychologically. If he is not personally infected by the
fear, then he will probably engage in a campaign of aggressive
tendencies to hold his own against the atmosphere of appre-
hension, or else he will attempt to escape the atmosphere of
the home as much as possible. As the child matures and finds
that these many fears surrounding his early years were without
reason, he will develop a confirmed disrespect for the advice,
influence, and discipline of the parent.

Bushnell was convinced that the parent must care for the
infant with a measure of trust and confidence, which is
grounded in a secure trust in God and a belief in the fullness of
life. This will gradually bring about a similar response on the
part of the child, helping him to form attitudes important to
wholesome behavior and a growing religious faith.

Bushnell seemed to recognize the power of what today is
called the subconscious mind. During the age of impressions,
the harsh attitudes and perverse feelings that the child experiences may develop into harmful feelings and unpleasant char-

acteristics. All the wholesome but unspoken influences during childhood, however, will bear their fruit as well. The seeds of character so important to religion, which were sown early, also begin to germinate. Bushnell comments:

> What they do not remember still remembers them, and now claims a right in them. What was before unconscious, flames into consciousness, and they break forth into praise and thanksgiving, in that which, long ago, took them initially, and touched them softly without thanks.[13]

THE BEGINNINGS OF DISCIPLINE

It may be thought, states Bushnell, that with all the emphasis on the plastic, impressionable nature of the infant, he has no will of his own. This is not true. He does not have a "responsible" will to the extent that he has a choice to make fully responsible decisions. He does have a will, nevertheless, that is strongly developed. "The manifestations of it are sometimes even frightful." Hence, even in this early age of impressions the matter of discipline becomes crucial.

It is a time when the child begins to learn to adjust to authority, to learn obedience to parents, to duty and religion, and to God. It is a time for beginning to fashion attitudes that will greatly affect his religious life in later years. This development of the child's ego-identity, of his independent and responsible will, is a gradual process extending over many years.

If a discipline of "terror and storm" is established, the child will either be psychologically broken down by fear or else be made a hundred times more obstinate. The proper objective is to school and to temper the child from the very beginning "to a customary self-surrender which takes nothing from his natural force and manliness." [14]

> The true problem is different; it is not to break, but *to bend* rather, to draw the will down, or away from self-

assertion toward self-devotion, to teach it the way of
submitting to wise limitations, and raise it into great
and glorious liberties of a state of loyalty to God.[15]

Bushnell recommends that when the very young child becomes obstinate the parent simply have him do what he is
supposed to do, as if he were capable of making no objection.
The parent is to do this again and again in a kindly way. Under such a wise influence the child will come to feel an obligation to obedience that does not break down his feeling of independence. This type of conduct is important for religious
conversion and a sense of allegiance to God later on in life.

He placed a strong emphasis on the discipline of children,
maintaining that it begins in the early stages of childhood when
the mother puts a little decision into the tones of her love.
This is the beginning of authority. Then comes the next phase:

> The stiffer tension of the masculine word, connected
> with the wider, rougher providence of a father's mascu-
> line force, follows in a stouter mode of authority, and
> the moral nature of the child, configured thereto, an-
> swers faithfully in a rapidly developed sense of obliga-
> tion.[16]

There should be order and regularity in the feeding of the
child to help establish other regular habits of life. Moderate
amounts of food and drink are to be given. Candy and rich
food should not be given a child to pacify the bursts of crying
or states of irritation. This not only puts undue emphasis upon
the taste sensation but also constitutes a reward for a fitful expression of self-will. Anything that unduly stimulates the appetite of the child may be instrumental in turning him into
a sensual, uninhibited person.

It was evident to Bushnell that many significant things were
happening in this age of impressions. "Let every Christian
father and mother understand, when their child is three years
old, they have done more than half of all they will ever do for
his character." [17]

TEACHING RELIGION

The attitudes and handling of the nursery have their implications for character and the later religious life. The atmosphere of the home, the consistency of spirit in all activities, the habit of good table manners, family prayers and hymns—these are the elements that make a strong initial impact on the child and shape his future.

The observance of Sunday in a special and wholesome manner builds an important foundation within the child; some simple teaching about God and his day may be given. Pictures and stories of Jesus as a friend and brother may be used.

While Bushnell does not elaborate on this theme, here is the faint beginning of modern-day nursery and kindergarten teaching with various playthings designed for feeling, looking, and doing. It is evident how his insights and doctrines of child nurture would soon lead to the developments of the twentieth century. These ideas are in startling contrast to the religious practices of his day, and are significant for their affinity to present-day ideas on child nurture.

31

chapter 3 IMPLICATIONS
OF NURTURE
FOR CHILDREN

Christian nurture was Bushnell's theme song. This was his great contribution to the life of the church in his time. He introduced a new humanizing quality to the treatment of children and their training.

It was Bushnell's opinion that a child is not really born until he has breathed a long time.[1] This was his way of distinguishing the stages of development. At first the child is almost wholly in the matrix of the parental will and attitude. Gradually the child develops his own will and begins to act as an independent self. Steadily the child passes from the "impression" stage to the stage of "responsible" action. The increasing power of language expresses an intellectual development in comparison to the purely emotional behaviors of infancy.[2]

When the child begins to feel his new powers and asserts his new selfhood in the obstinate and rebellious modes noted in the previous chapter, he is moving into the wonderful adventures of childhood. Here is the dawning of new intellectual powers that grow with his ability to use words and ideas which express his feelings, impressions, and attitudes.

Bushnell stated that "a child acts out his present feelings of the moment, without qualification or disguise." [3] And again he noted that "children love the realities, and are worried by shams of character." [4] The child develops unerring ability to gauge and to feel the reality and consistency in parents and in people. He is able to sense any inconsistency or pretension.

When children have been raised within a religious environment, they "have many times of great religious tenderness, when they are drawn apart in thoughtfulness and prayer." [5] There is in childhood a natural tendency for awe and wonder, for meditation, as the youngster seeks after meanings in the great new world opening up before him. These natural moods are to be used and enhanced. They are not to be hindered or spoiled. The family atmosphere should be congenial and supportive to these moods. Here are opportunities for parents to help make their children aware of the presence of God.

Remembering rustic scenes of his youthful days on the farm when colts, calves, and lambs frolicked upon green fields on warm spring mornings, he wrote: "Having set the young of all the animal races a playing, and made their beginning an age of frisking life and joyous gambol, it would be singular if God had made the young of humanity an exception." [6]

There is a need for children to play. This was a fresh note in New England, which had a heritage of rather austere religion. Instead of a symptom of original sin, this play of children was an appointment of God with real educational value. He saw in it a symbol of the true liberty of the Christian life. Since play has no motive but play, so Christian goodness will have no motive but to be good in the relationship with God. He concluded with this significant statement:

> As play is the forerunner of religion, so religion is to be the friend of play; to love its free motion, its happy scenes, its voices of glee, and never, by any needless austerities of control, seek to hamper and shorten its pleasures. [7]

There is a danger that religion will be introduced to the child solely in the form of restriction to the effect that " God requires of you this, forbids you in that." While obedience and law has its place in religion, Bushnell contends that it must not be presented to the child wholly in the form of constraint or it soon takes on a repulsive look. When the attractive elements are accentuated, then gradually obedience will fit into religion in such a way that its value will be recognized. Hence, he stressed the importance of children enjoying the various festivals and important days of the Christian year.

He urged parents to take particular cognizance of the need to be interested in the play of children. He recommended those strenuous out-of-doors games "that give sprightliness and robustness to the body." Parents should prepare games and projects for long evenings and bad weather so that the house does not become a prison, but instead a cheerful, attractive place.

He further advised parents not to be disturbed unduly by the child if "by mere exuberance of life, he is occasionally hurried away from the sacred things, into matters of play." [8] He can understand when they show restlessness in the Sunday service and signs of wanting to escape. For these natural inclinations parents are not to scold the children, saying that they do not love God. Even adults are often thinking about some journey or business deal during the sermon.

GROWING INDEPENDENCE

The growing independence of the child is a central fact with which parents must cope. Whereas the infant was more properly a "candidate for personality," the child is becoming a real person. Bushnell compares the child to a seed that forms in the capsule of the parent stem, getting all its sustenance and characteristics from the stem. Imperceptibly and gradually the seed ripens, then separates and falls off in a complete form of life by itself. This is a transition that continues over many years, and the nurture that is influential in this transition will have significant and external results.

AUTHORITY AND DISCIPLINE

The task of bending the will to learn obedience, rather than breaking it, is begun in infancy. This task continues on through

34

childhood even though it be in diminishing degree. The child continues to feel out his powers, to explore the limitations of life, and to come to terms with authority. Parents must exercise a certain pressure of control and restriction of law upon the moral nature of the child, although it may not always be welcome. They must exercise a real authority and a true "family government."

If parents fail to carry out this exercise of discipline in child-training because of sentimentality or neglect or lack of understanding, "there is no greater cruelty . . . than this same false tenderness, which is the bane of so many families." [9] Equally cruel is family discipline characterized by "that brutish manner of despotic will and violence," which relies on fear and force, making no appeal to the moral nature of the child at all. It is not sufficient that parents sacrifice themselves, lavish devotion, advise and exhort, feed and dress their children. They need to implement that particular idea of family government which is "that it governs, uses authority, maintains law and rules, by a binding and loosing power, over the moral nature of the child." [10]

Bushnell sees this family discipline and government as an authority set up by God. He even goes so far as to say that the parents are to be "personating God in the child's feeling and conscience, and bending it, thus, to what . . . we call a filial piety." [11] Since God has set children within families instead of creating them as outright, independent persons, this family relationship is symbolic of the higher relationship with God. No parent, however, has the right to misuse his authority so as to turn it into an oppression that allows no liberty or self-dignity to the youngster.

Bushnell offers specific suggestions for the parent in giving commands. They should be given in a quiet, meaningful voice and will be effective if the parent is consistent in backing up what he has said. "The violent emphasis, the hard stormy voice, the menacing air, only *weakens* authority." He vividly describes the parents who rave from morning until night without seeing that the commands are carried out:

Their mandates follow so thickly as to crowd one another, and even successively to thrust one another out
of remembrance. And the result is that, by this can-
nonading of popguns, the successive pellets of com-
mandment are in turn all blown away.[12]

Too many prohibitions discourage and oppress the child,
building up a resistance and disobedience to all commandments.
Again, Bushnell portrays the situation with sharp detail:

There is a monotony of continuous, ever-sounding pro-
hibition, which is really awful. It does not stop with
ten commandments, like the word of Sinai, but it keeps
the thunder up, from day to day, saying always thou
shalt not do this, nor this, nor this, till, in fact, there
is really nothing left to be done. The whole enjoy-
ment, use, benefit of life is quite used up by the prohibitions. The child lives under the tilt-hammer of com-
mandment, beaten to the ground as fast as he attempts
to rise.[13]

There are good suggestions in Bushnell's *Christian Nurture*
about the punishment of children. He firmly believes in it but
hastens to make explicit the wisdom with which it is to be dispensed. It, too, is to be threatened as seldom as possible. "It
is a most wretched and coarse barbarity that turns the house into
a penitentiary, or house of correction." [14] Such punishments
are to be severe enough to accomplish their purpose but gentle
enough to show the concern and love of the parent.

After the "sad necessity" has arisen, time needs to be taken
to produce a calm attitude and an objective evaluation on the
part of the parent. The punishment needs to be carried out
in private where family members and other persons will not be
present, so as to spare the self-respect of the child. The disci-
plinary measures are not to be discontinued until the desired
change has been accomplished. It is not sufficient to let the
child go sulking away with a defiant look that indicates a will-

fulness not yet subdued. The real point of the discipline is not carried "till the child is softened into love and duty; sorry, in all heartiness, for the past, with a glad mind set to the choice of doing right and pleasing God." [15] Bushnell does agree, however, that occasionally an "explosion" is warranted when some shocking misconduct occurs, whereupon the father shouts some terrible outburst of righteous indignation. Very likely Bushnell is here recalling a memorable experience in his own boyhood.

Once again Bushnell's profound psychological insight becomes evident when he states that parents are not to continue their displeasure too long in the administration of punishment. After the wrong has been visibly recognized and repented by the child, the parent must not go on as though bearing a grudge. This prolongation of punishment, this continuance of anger, this pressure of displeasure, this pretending of a diminuation of love, becomes a very serious threat to the child. He may fail to comprehend the reason for this attitude and become very confused and insecure. Or, the child may become so discouraged by this withholding of love that he will learn to get along without it.

When the child begins to show even tokens of repentance the parent should hasten to the child "in glad recognitions and cordial greetings," in order to heal the pain of the incident. He refers to the prodigal's father in the parable of Jesus and sees in it a representation of the great generosity of God toward men. If this is the nature of God's attitude toward the parents, it is the manner in which they must treat their children. [16] In exercising their authority, parents are always to retain love, patience, and a sense of humor.

Parents are to understand, nevertheless, that parental government is to culminate in the emancipation of the child. This process should begin early and progress imperceptibly. Parents are not to maintain a total and unyielding authority until the last possible moment and then give sudden and complete freedom to their youth. They are to begin early to let the child practice and develop his use of responsibility and independence. [17]

37

Bushnell realizes that children are not to be made Christians by the rod. There are no shortcuts for establishing piety and religious faith in children. They should be encouraged to do right because it is right, not because wrongdoing is not safe or does not look good. This genuine spirit of obedience within a Christian family can have a great deal to do with the development of a child into a Christian person. Indeed, Bushnell would classify family government as a "converting ordinance" just as important as preaching.

HABIT FORMATION

Bushnell could see that wholeness and beauty of character should be started early in life. Those who become Christians in their later years have a great struggle, because all their old habits are warring against their new motivations and against their new loyalty to Christ. Moral character takes a long time to develop in its real strength and highest quality. This was why Bushnell could not countenance the neglect of children until they were of the age to be converted.

Habits of prayer need to be established in childhood. There should be a regular practice of saying table graces in a family atmosphere where prayer and a sense of God's presence are well known. The child should be taught to pray for himself by speaking sentence prayers or little formulas suited to his age. Later he may express inner feelings with spontaneous prayers.

In the whole manner of training and establishing good habits for the Christian life, it is necessary that children be shown how to be good. When they fail in this they need to understand that God will help them if they trust in him and ask him for help. In a way, children pass through little conversion-like crises all the time and gradually draw nearer to God. Bushnell advises:

> Let them be accustomed to it as a fact of experience that they are happy when they are right, and are right when God helps them to be, and that he always helps them to be when they put their trust in him.[18]

THE FAMILY ATMOSPHERE

It is essential that the family religion be in agreement with the other attitudes, objectives, and practices of the family. Children perceive the inconsistencies and may pick up attitudes and actions of the parents that belie the religious faith they profess.

As an example, there is the father who prays every morning that his children may grow up as good Christians living unto God; then he rushes to his office or shop where he works and feverishly acts all day as if the one motive in his life were that of becoming rich. The mother, by her preferences and opinions, may act in strong contradiction to the father's prayers. Or it may be that both parents are involved with ambitions for social standing, envying those in a higher income bracket, and concerned with the social status of their sons and daughters. All such reasons may contradict the religious beliefs of the family.

Inadvertently, the children absorb the faults and good points of their parents. If the mother is a scandalmonger, her children will soon become gossipers. If the mother puts great emphasis on fashion, show, and dress, the youngsters will soon catch a spirit of pride and vanity. If the home is disorganized and untidy, this becomes a way of life for the children. When the parents are ill-tempered and impatient, the children acquire the same disposition. If inappropriate activities are carried out on Sunday, the children will follow that example. When parents laugh at religion, this is reason enough for the children to find fault with it. Bushnell believes that Christian nurture must take place within the family circle, where its influence is the most important for the life of the child.

QUALIFICATION OF PARENTS

The fulfillment of true fatherhood and motherhood is impossible unless the parents be Christians themselves: "Have it first in yourselves, then teach it as you live it; teach it by living it; for you can do it in no other manner."[19]

A careful self-discipline on the part of the parents is an essential part of the Christian family life. It may be easy for some parents to resort to use of the rod alone, or to inflict brute force or dictatorship. Those parents who "batter and bruise the delicate, tender souls of their children, extinguishing in them what they ought to cultivate," have no Christian nurture or true family discipline. Rather, the authority and rule of the parents must be rooted in righteousness and love.

Bushnell was perturbed that, while many professions require an apprenticeship or a thorough training, parents so often approach their tremendous task with no preparation whatsoever—indeed, without even much conviction that they need preparation. Some young mothers undertake their sacred office to govern, manage, and teach their children according to their own whims, feelings, and tempers of the moment, based upon what they have chanced to experience. In recent years churches have begun to provide counseling services, training courses, and books for young parents.[20]

Bushnell suggests that parents should speak occasionally to children about their own faults and weak points. They can acknowledge to their children that they themselves are struggling with weaknesses and feel sorry for their sins, but know that God will forgive.

Such a practice will accomplish two things. First, it will give a realistic and true picture of the parents, so that when the child passes from the stage of hero-worship of the parent into the new stage of realism, and is able to perceive the parental foibles for himself, he will not be so greatly disillusioned.[21] Second, this practice will attract the friendly sympathy of the children toward the parent. To acknowledge and deplore the mixture of evil that will be blended within the family life is the best way to deal with the matter. Thus, the whole family may unite in a common effort to rise above evil and selfishness, to live the Christian life.

IMPARTING THE FAITH

Bushnell speaks—in a manner typical of the modern kindergarten teacher—about ways of engendering positive feeling tones toward family, church, Sunday, Jesus, and God. For the children who are very young and whose emotional capacities are predominant, he suggests pictures and stories and the "playthings of the hands and eyes." He knows the readiness of children to respond to games and drills which are set to music. He suggests that the parent or teacher encourage the children to invent their own play and games where they learn about relationships through taking turns, and through interchange one with the other. It is a time when the parent needs to watch the moods of the children, sharing their happy and humorous moments, drawing them out of their discouragements, supporting them in periods of frustrations and weakness, noting their reactions of awe and wonderment, and thus guiding them appropriately into Christian ways of living.

Bushnell further suggests that children who are growing older and whose intellectual capacities are increasing are in a period when "playthings of the mind" come into use—books, pictures, hymns. It is a time for friendly conversations about God and Christ, dealing with the beauty and order of creation, which manifests God's wisdom and greatness. Such conversation will show God as a friendly and attractive being, rather than a God of severities and terrors. There may be interesting discussions and inquiries carried on concerning Christ as a child, as a brother, as a friend. In addition, it should be mentioned that Jesus truly loved children, that he talked to them and often took them upon his knee, and that he said, "Of such is the kingdom of heaven."

Bushnell did not believe that small children should be "worried and drummed into apathy by dogmatic catechisms." He favored the use of the Lord's Prayer, the Ten Commandments, the Apostles' Creed or the Nicene Creed, hymns, and facts of the gospel. These would be more interesting and meaningful to children than the interpretations and opinions of the catechism. Theology could not be explicitly taught to children, but the central essence of such theology could be taught implicitly.

The life and teaching of Christ was a truly central element for teaching. Here was God's truth put into concrete form.

By studying the dramatic events in the life of Jesus Christ, children could see and comprehend the core of the gospel. The use of a good map is helpful to set forth all the natural topography and geography of the Holy Land where the patriarchs and prophets lived and where miracles and battles took place. Such incidents of the Bible stories could be told with great interest and variety.

The child is not to be reproved for asking questions, because his curiosity and eagerness to learn are very important for his whole outlook on life. Hasty answers that may need to be retracted, or which may prove inconsistent and faulty should not be given. Parents will often have to explain that many of God's mysteries in the world are too deep for the human mind, and that much in life has to be taken in faith.

Frequently there may be interesting conversations with the children about the church and the sacraments or related topics. The church may be described as "God's holy family, or school, in which all the members are disciples or learners together." In this church Christ himself is present, the unseen teacher and Lord. It should be impressed upon the child that he himself is a member of this holy family and that Christ accepted the church and grew up as a disciple within it. Thus, the child will be caught up into the cause and spirit of church family, even as in his own family. The sacrament of baptism will be set forth to him as a sacred event in his life. Here was the promise of continuing, cleansing, restoring grace from God extended to him.

Horace Bushnell graded methods and materials to suit the various age-groups in the instruction of Christian truth. His ideas for parents in teaching and nurturing their children within the family circle can be easily adapted for use in church schools. Indeed, a reminder is frequently needed that this man, who sounds so akin to the educators in our present-day churches, wrote his theories more than a century ago.

chapter 4 THE DILEMMA
CRYING FOR
A SOLUTION

Horace Bushnell proved to be the champion of children in the life of the church. Indeed, such a champion had been needed for more than a century and a half within the pioneer churches of New England.

As Calvinism strove to adapt itself to the changing patterns of life in a new country, it became customary for children to find themselves in a most abnormal situation within the context of the Christian church. The child was either "forced" to enter religion in the same manner as an adult, or wait until an age of maturity when he could know a conversion experience. The latter idea was much in vogue in the early nineteenth century. Both alternatives were equally unhappy. It was indeed urgent that someone come to the rescue and dignify the position of children in the Christian religion in America.

THE EARLY PURITAN CHURCH

As the Puritan settlers established their unique form of theocratic government in the New England colonies, they eventually had to settle upon a guiding standard of doctrine. The

43

document formulated in 1648, later known as the Cambridge Platform, became a constitution for the churches. It accepted the theology of the Westminster Confession of Faith, which had finally been passed in 1647 in Britain. A further doctrinal affirmation made at the Saybrook Synod of Connecticut in 1708 remained for a long time the doctrinal statement of the churches of New England.

Divine sovereignty was a central doctrine of Calvin's system of theology. God was thought of as an absolute and irresistable sovereign, his government and control extending over all things. God had mercy on some and hardened his heart against others. The doctrine had implications for what were called "decrees"—decrees of election and reprobation. Since everything must happen according to God's will, God had predetermined that some would be saved to eternal salvation and others sent to eternal damnation and punishment.

In contrast to God's sovereignty was the inherent depravity of the human soul, which was preached with earnest insistence. Jonathan Edwards is reported to have said: "The heart is like a viper, hissing, and spitting poison at God"; and again, "The malice of damned spirits is but a branch of the root that is in the hearts of natural men now." Man was thought to be involved in a complete helplessness in his sin. He had no ability to repent, to turn to God, or to do anything good on his own power. He must wait for God to move him before he could turn to God. He could do nothing for himself and his own salvation.

Church membership and baptism soon became disturbing problems. In these new theocracies everyone was compelled to attend church, but not everyone could qualify for church membership, which brought with it full privileges within the community. The churches insisted upon the public confession of the candidate's spiritual experience and his knowledge of the principles of religion. Many people who were eager to become full members were unable to give such accounts. The letters of membership from churches in England were often refused. Much dissatisfaction developed among those of Congregational descent and those of no connection. With the influx of new settlers and the growth of a second generation the problems increased.

THE HALFWAY COVENANT

For the "sturdy souls" who were sifted out of the Puritan and Separatist movements in England and Holland to make up the first contingent of settlers to New England, it was not unnatural to impose a strict test for church membership. This was partly a reaction against the formal confession of the European state church system. An earnest attempt was made to prevent anyone who had not experienced regeneration from entering the church. It became such a trying ordeal that people soon chose to forgo communion rather than go through such an exacting test in the presence of a congregation of people.

The result was a serious decline in church membership, which meant a decrease in the number of citizens with full voting privileges. A compromise solution to the difficulty was worked out by a Ministerial Convention in 1657. The decision became known as the Halfway Covenant and was reaffirmed by a synod meeting in 1662.

It stated that those who believed in God and acknowledged his claims upon their lives, if they promised submission to the discipline of the church, might bring their children to be baptized even though they could not profess conversion. However, neither they nor their children could be admitted to the Lord's table without a profession of regeneration.[1]

These factors illustrate the deep roots of the problem that Horace Bushnell had to face. With the advent of the Great Awakening in the middle-eighteenth century, renewed emphasis was put upon this cataclysmic type of conversion experience, together with a strict testing of new members. This overemphasis on one part of Calvinism began to obscure the meaning and significance of another part; namely, the doctrine of the covenant. Originally the churches of Calvinistic persuasion had maintained the covenant relationship with God as the basis for vital membership within the church of the children of Christian believers. The doctrine concerning the place of children in the church had become confused. Doctrine and practice were not consistent.

THE GREAT AWAKENING (1740–43)

The long awaited and much prayed for spiritual quickening began in 1734 at Northampton, Massachusetts, under the ministry of Jonathan Edwards. Within a year, more than three hundred persons had been converted. Small revivals began to occur in various places and before long the Great Awakening was under way. A similar movement among the Presbyterians in New Jersey was begun by the elder William Tennant and was continued by his four sons, of whom Gilbert Tennant became most renowned. The revivalistic tours in the colonies by George Whitefield of England, plus his contact with both Edwards and Tennant, helped to set the movement under way. It reached its peak proportions from 1740 to 1742 when twenty-five thousand to fifty thousand new members were added to the New England churches.

During this period the Calvinistic theory that conversion was totally the work of God alone continued to be upheld. Nevertheless, a doctrine was evolving in which new stress was placed upon human responsibility. It was being recognized that there were certain "means" which might be used to help the soul "into position" to receive the regenerating work of God's spirit. As the techniques of revivalistic preaching were perfected for the persuasion of great numbers, this became more evident. While it was always said that such quickenings were the work of God's spirit, it was accepted that revivalistic preachers became more effective in their campaigns when little was said about the election of God. Many preachers ignored the paradox of preaching predestination to life or to death, while at the same time inviting sinners to flee from wrath and to accept life.

In the preaching of the Great Awakening, a powerful attempt was made to bring the people "under conviction." This conviction involved three factors: a vivid comprehension of sin and the miseries due to it, a distressing sense of one's own sin, a great despair within oneself that relief from this distressing sense might never come. Feeling utterly helpless as an abominable sinner, one had no assurance that God would help him or that God had elected him to receive salvation.

As the Great Awakening progressed, the terrors of an angry and wrathful God were sermonized by the preachers to bring about conviction to unbelievers of the horrors and torment of hellfire. In such sermons the preacher had to raise his voice to a crescendo to be heard above the weeping and hysterical screams of women.

A classic example was Jonathan Edwards' sermon "Sinners in the Hands of an Angry God," which he preached to his congregation at Northampton, Massachusetts, and again at Enfield, Connecticut, in July, 1741. An excerpt from that sermon proclaims:

> The God that holds you over the pit of hell much as one holds a spider, or some loathesome insect, over the fire, abhors you, and is dreadfully provoked. . . . And yet it is nothing but his hand that holds you from falling into the fire every moment. It is ascribed to nothing else that you did not go to hell last night. . . . It would be a wonder if some that are now present should not be in hell in a very short time, before this year is out. And it would be no wonder if some persons that now sit here in some seats of this meetinghouse in health and quiet, and secure, should be there before tomorrow morning.[2]

This sort of preaching had a powerful impact upon adults, but unfortunately children were also subjected to it. It was believed that children, too, must have this soul-rending experience of conversion if they were to become Christians. Children were treated as miniature adults and no distinction was made between childhood and adulthood.

An appeal to fear as a motive to forsake sin and to seek salvation was considered legitimate even with children. From earliest childhood vivid descriptions of judgment and hell were branded upon their fertile imaginations. They were constantly warned of the momentary danger of hell and ceaselessly exhorted to accept salvation. The whole situation became even more tragic when children were forced to undergo the anguish of "conviction," yet without any assurance that God had elected them or would assist them. In addition, to be consistent with the required steps for conversion, little children were forced to admit that they were "willing to be damned for God's sake."

In a criticism of the revivals, a minister named Charles Chauncy referred to an article that indicated the hysteria caused by revivalists using a shouting voice in their preaching of judgment: "This frequently frightens the Little Children, and sets them a Screaming; and that frights their tender Mothers, and sets them to Screaming, and by Degrees spreads [over] a great part of the Congregation." [3]

The excesses that accompanied some of the revivals caused sharp contention that resulted in a division in the Congregational churches. Jonathan Edwards published a book in which he defended or at least made allowances for some of these excesses. He was answered by an opposing treatise written in 1743 by Charles Chauncy, who was more liberal in doctrine. There quickly arose two parties. The "New Lights" favored revivals, the dramatic oratory of itinerant preachers, and an emotional experience as the only proof of the Christian life. The "Old Light" party opposed revival emotionalism, questioned the permanence of the work of itinerant evangelists, and preferred the ordinary means of grace for securing Christian discipleship.

This division among the ministers and churches also led to doctrinal differences; the New Lights tended to become the orthodox wing and the Old Lights tended to become the liberal wing. The liberal school was inclined to put more emphasis on the use of human "means" in bringing people to God. Indeed, it was from this liberal wing that the Unitarian movement broke away in the early 1800's.

48

The theories of Edwards are significant because he introduced into Calvinism an assertion of man's responsibility, though he made a careful distinction between man's "moral ability" and his "natural ability." In 1754 he wrote a book on this topic, *A Careful and Strict Enquiry into the Modern Prevailing Notions of Freedom of Will.* In it he maintained that human freedom implies simply the natural power to act in accordance with the choice of mind. God must reveal himself to man as his highest good, thus rendering the choice of obedience to God as man's strongest determination.

There developed an "Edwardean" school of ministers composed of friends and followers of Edwards who defended, revised, and elaborated on his doctrines and ideas. There were also many writers who opposed his doctrines and presented other views. Sermons, rebuttals, and controversies continued within this period of doctrinal ferment.

THE SECOND GREAT AWAKENING (1797–1801, 1812–13)

The triumphs and successes of the Great Awakening were short-lived. Because of the sharp reaction over the excesses, plus a natural weariness after a period of such high religious excitement, the awakening came to a close in 1743. Itinerant preachers were banned from regular pulpits. Jonathan Edwards' own congregation was apathetic and not one new member was received in four years. He was dismissed by them in Northhampton during a dispute.

The majority of ministers belonged to the Old Light party and promptly put away all revivalistic practices. Church memberships were declining and the ministers were not very strict about the admission of new members or the discipline of recalcitrant ones. The bitter doctrinal controversies did not help the vitality of the churches. Moreover, the political, economic, and military situation was disturbed and unsettled from 1755 to 1789. In that period occurred the outbreak of the Revolution of 1775, the Declaration of Independence, and the final establishment of government under the Constitution. Consequently, religion was at low ebb.

During this period the ministers of the Old Light school failed to give relevant leadership in a troubled time. Preaching was indifferent and boring, with no special attempt made to interest youth, and family visitations practically ceased. Irreligion and immorality grew to serious proportions.

Gradually the New Light school of ministers increased their numbers and control in New England. They were noted for their strictness of discipline and their careful examination of new members concerning the nature of their religious experience. Because of their strictness their popularity increased slowly. By 1796 there were more than a hundred ministers in the New Light group, the majority of whom were in Connecticut. Significantly, Timothy Dwight of the Edwardean theology was elected to the presidency of Yale College in 1795.

Under Dwight, Yale College was rejuvenated and Dwight made a pointed and effective attack upon the appalling conditions of irreligion both in the college and in New England. He did much to set the pace for the New Light men. Revivals were favored to build up the churches and the pastors created a powerful moral and spiritual force with their warm, evangelical preaching.

Dwight demurred against the theology of some of his predecessors and tended to be more moderate and conciliatory. He advocated the use of "means" and maintained that the unconverted man was better for his good deeds and his attempts at obedience to God. He developed a more commonsense combination of "dependence upon God and personal responsibility."

By 1798 the Second Great Awakening was under way. Various factors contributed to this development. Widespread alarm had arisen that the very foundations of society were threatened by the proportions of immorality and irreligion. There arose a strong reaction against the deism of Europe, and against the atheistic ideas stemming from the French Revolution.

A surprising number of the capable, vigorous ministers, now known as "New Divinity" men, entered pastorates in the

1790's and were especially concentrated in Litchfield County. It was here that the Second Awakening became most widespread and influential. Horace Bushnell was born in this same Litchfield County in 1802.

The idea of "disinterested benevolence," which had developed within New England Calvinism, provided a wholesome expression for the renewed religious interest of the time. Church members began to enter into various humanitarian works; joined missionary activities; and distributed tracts, Sunday school literature, and Bibles. As a result a new interest in spiritual matters revitalized the churches in New England.

Certainly there were significant trends and changes taking place in the practices of those churches in the era of the Second Awakening. But what was the fate of the children during all the years of revival? For one thing, the meetings were not the emotional orgies and devastating experiences of the Great Awakening. Nevertheless, the earnest, steady preaching of the basic Calvinistic doctrines must have had a powerfully disturbing effect on children's minds. A climactic conversion experience was still the only way that a child could come into the Christian life. The experience of "conviction" was still a fearful thing to the children, just as hell was a grim reality to them.

A NEW MOOD IN RELIGION

Another important revisionist of Congregational doctrine was Nathaniel W. Taylor (1786–1858). Having studied under Timothy Dwight, he served a pastorate in New Haven and was appointed the first professor of theology at Yale Divinity College. Here he exerted a powerful influence until his death.

Taylor was convinced that God had made man a free agent and the corollary of freedom was the power to sin. God wanted man to choose holiness and gave him free agency to do it; the power to sin was an incidental part of such freedom. Sinfulness or moral depravity was therefore not created in man; it did not consist in duplicating Adam's act; it was a universal tendency or disposition. It was man's own act constituted in a free choice of some object rather than God as his chief good.

This new doctrine of man's freedom was too much for the conservative members of Congregationalism. Under the leadership of Bennet Tyler, they initiated strong opposition. A theological seminary was set up—now Hartford Theological Seminary—whose sole purpose was to oppose and to correct this heresy. Thus began the famous Taylor-Tyler controversy.

Horace Bushnell studied theology under Nathaniel Taylor; and although he was influenced by Taylor's system of theology, he was never in full sympathy with it.

The religious phase of the revolt was gaining momentum. It was a time of strong advance by the Unitarians. The liberal theology of men like Chauncy, Mayhew, and Briant had been growing in influence, especially in eastern Massachusetts. By the end of the Revolution (1776), many Massachusetts ministers openly denied the depravity of man, publicly opposed the doctrine of eternal punishment, and expressed anti-Trinitarian ideas. The Second Great Awakening brought a resurgence of conservative doctrine.

Because of the threat from the Unitarians, Taylor had to reframe Calvinist ideas into a practical, preachable theology. His stress on man's free agency proved similar to that of Lyman Beecher and Charles G. Finney. Indeed, he joined forces with Lyman Beecher in an effort to stop the inroads of the Unitarians and to win recruits back to the Congregational fold.

The revivals continued, since they were supported by the theology of the conservative as well as the moderate parties of Congregationalism. They included the preaching of regeneration as a climactic experience.

The conservative element maintained the same rigorous and harsh attitude toward the conversion of children. Tyler never relented from the position that the child was an enemy of God, that the soul's corruption was inalienable, that no attractive or gradual impressions could draw it from its depravity.

A CHANGING SOCIETY

There were also economic transitions and social revolts in progress at this time. A new class of prosperous merchants and professional men was rising up with the gradual shift to trade and industry from an agrarian type of economy. In large centers like Boston a new social caste developed. Possessing new wealth and security, these people achieved new elegance and comfort in their standards of living, new refinement in their intellectual and literary tastes. To such persons in their new power and elegance the strict doctrines of Calvinism became increasingly repugnant; they were not easily convinced that they were helpless pawns in the hands of Calvin's arbitrary God. From the plain meetinghouses and the long sermons on "total depravity" there was a large exodus to the more aesthetic and liturgical churches of Episcopalianism, or else to the more intellectually liberal Unitarian congregations.

Those of the new cultural classes who remained Congregationalists tended to ignore theological dogmas. On Sunday they outwardly maintained the appearance of Calvinists, but on weekdays they were actually rationalists. Large numbers were becoming totally indifferent to the church.

In the past, Puritan practices and Calvinistic theologies have been indiscriminately compared with Bushnell's doctrine of Christian nurture. This was an incomplete and inaccurate picture. The research of recent years has given a much more realistic picture of the flux and tension in the social situation in which Bushnell did his creative work.[4]

As a result of the social mobility of the time certain tensions became apparent. Parents fearfully watched their sons and daughters migrate to the city with its many temptations and different social patterns. In the sophisticated, urban classes parents were concerned with the dissipation and escapades of their youth. Cut off from familiar moorings, the young people were painfully in need of guidance and reassurance. Out of the "emotional duress" of this flux there developed a new literature. The home was idealized as the symbol of security, religion, and moral strength.

This background of temptation, irreligion, and wickedness of a changing culture prompted many people to look back wistfully to the simplicity of their childhood days. This backward longing and its associations helped to put children in new prominence and to make them objects of increased understanding. Although many adults were indifferent to religion for their own sakes, they avidly clutched at religion for the sake of their children, hoping it might bring stability and direction for the uncertain future. A few writers in religious journals began to question the practice of attributing so much depravity to children. They began to advocate a more moderate and understanding approach toward the Christian education of the younger generation.

Moreover, in this period the mother was highly esteemed and often glorified as a "key to salvation" because she, like the child, was exempt from the competitive struggles of commerce and political life. She ruled in the quiet haven of the home and she possessed tremendous powers of influence for the crucial years of childhood.

Because of the perplexing social problems and the breakup of old family patterns, people became hungry for counseling. They were in need of a fresh directive that would integrate the insights of their new psychology with a realistic theology capable of commanding the allegiance of both mind and heart. Horace Bushnell, minister at Hartford, was the man who came forth with a creative synthesis.

chapter 5 RISING
TO THE
CHALLENGE

As a youth Bushnell adopted the orthodox Calvinist views that were preached in the little country church his parents attended. Because his father was a Methodist and his mother Episcopalian, there was within the Bushnell home a quiet resistance to the total depravity and the predestination doctrines which were stressed at church. This attitude probably helped him to make a radical break from such beliefs in later years.

At the age of seventeen, he had written a paper examining these Calvinist doctrines and attempting to prove that Paul must have been mistaken when he "wishes himself accursed from Christ for his brethren." [1] This sounds like a strong reaction to a proof text used to support the typical conversion test of "being willing to be damned for God's sake." At Divinity School he was not in accord with Nathaniel Taylor's logical system of theology. As a young minister he was forced by the problems of his pastorate to examine the attitude he should take toward the prevalent practice of relying upon revivals as the sole measure of religious life. He was forced by circumstances to make a restudy of the assumptions and doctrines current in the life of the church.

THE GROWING PRESSURES

As a young minister, Bushnell knew constant pressure and frustration. The people of Hartford were becoming increasingly fastidious and sophisticated as a new cultural and economic class developed. North Congregational Church, Hartford, had originated as a splinter group from the congregation pastored by Joel Hawes, who was noted for his revivalistic emphasis. Bushnell became the third minister to a congregation divided in two by the Taylor-Tyler controversy.

He came into this difficult situation with no theological system of his own in a day when systems were the standard equipment of ministers. He came to his pastorate with an imperative Christian "experience" rather than a formulated theology, plus a determination to find "the truth" as he went along. The people were becoming more and more indifferent to religion and to preaching. Because of the insecurity of the social transition many of the upper classes were attracted to the Episcopal church. Others returned, uneasily, to the revivalism of Hawes' church as they sought some form of security and stability in the familiar religious pattern of former days. Bushnell was threatened with the possibility of a shrinking congregation. Ministers were measured by the number of yearly conversions.

Bushnell hoped for revival in his church and sought to prepare his people for it through preaching; he prayed for a quickening but it did not come. He also perceived the danger of successful revivals. It was customary for the local minister to be blamed for the letdown period that always followed a revival. For several years new members and baptisms were few in number at his church. He had begun his ministry at the age of thirty-one and now ten years had gone by with few results to show. He probably felt frustration as a result of his limited recognition and insignificant accomplishments.

REVIVALS APPRAISED

Bushnell's first publication was a sermon entitled "Crisis of the Church," which was printed in 1835. It was against slavery, though not abolitionist in nature. One of his first printed articles was "The Influence of Religion upon Your Health," printed in the *Quarterly Christian Spectator*, VIII (1836). This title was rather misleading because Bushnell was actually reviewing a book written by a phrenologist who had made disparaging remarks about religion and its effects upon health.

His next venture in publication was an 1838 article "The Spiritual Economy of Revivals," also printed in the *Quarterly Christian Spectator*.[2] Here he undertook to ascertain the real place of revivals in the divine plan. His attitude at this time was influenced by his own conversion, which had changed the course of his life in the Yale revival.

After a thorough study of the merits and disagreeable elements of revivals, Bushnell decided that the ministers themselves needed to acquire a more proportioned sense of character, to change the tone of their message, and to test the state of their people instead of preaching only repentance. He commented: "By this confined method, this continual beating on the same spot, they only produce a sense of soreness, which recoils from their attempts."[3]

GERMINAL IDEAS OF NURTURE

Gradually Bushnell became involved with the problems of the day as the pressures and discouragements of his pastorate continued. He now had children of his own. The popular literature stressed a new approach to children and called for a redefinition of religion. Bushnell keenly realized the need, for he was caught between the compromises of the day and the remnants of a meaningful faith.

In 1844 Bushnell published another article that was printed in *The New Englander*.[4] Entitled "The Kingdom of Heaven as a Grain of Mustard Seed," it was of major significance. It contained his fundamental principles of Christian nurture. His later works were an elaboration and expansion of these germinal ideas. He began the article with his famous analogy:

> To roll a snowball and to grow an oak are not the same thing. Enlargement of volume is a result in both cases;

but beyond this, they have nothing in common. In one, the result is wrought by an external force; in the other, by a vital force within.[5]

Bushnell claimed that this basic distinction held in reference to every organic and vital being. Growth must come from an inner activity or internal capacity for self-enlargement, whereby new matter is carefully selected, taken up internally, and assimilated into the organic whole. Bushnell believed this was true of the mind as it was of the animal or vegetable nature. Intellectual maturity must come from the internal activity of the mind itself and not from any outward accumulation. This also applied to the inner character of the Christian:

> So also with piety or Christian character. It must be a growth. Its increase and beauty must be wrought by the activity of spiritual life. Fires will not burn it into the soul. Statutes and penalities will not force it. Self-tortures and penances will as little avail. Sacraments and formal observances will not, of themselves, accomplish more.[6]

Then Bushnell proceeded to describe the nature of the growth of Christian character. This became the basic conception upon which his doctrine of Christian nurture stood:

> Its being is its life as a *spiritual creature of God*, quickened by his light and warmed by his love. Its volume is in its exercise, its aims and objects, *its internal struggles and conquests*; by which it grows up into him in whom it lives, showing first the blade, then the ear, and after that the full corn in the ear.[7]

APPRAISING THE CHURCH

Bushnell's exposition mentions that often when the inner spiritual life of the church wanes, the church turns to external forms and devices to accomplish the purpose it seeks. "The church in fact becomes a great ecclesiastical factory," he wrote, "running its thousand wheels to shape and polish and rub and grind the people into Christian disciples." [8]

Bushnell might well be describing the contemporary church. It is easy to forget he was writing a century ago. Bushnell makes clear that he does not advocate that the church become inactive or ingrown; its expansion and aggressiveness must issue from the spiritual life that comes from a close relationship with God. In a day when there were many benevolent societies, missionary groups, and book associations, piety had become synonymous with action. He indicates that the spirit of "our principle" requires every activity to proceed from within and forbids all substitutes for Christian piety.

> It commands the church first of all to live—demands of every Christian, who will add strength to the cause of Christ in the world, that he contribute first of all a holy life. It declares that bustle cannot save the world. [9]

CHILDREN IN THE CHURCH

Bushnell held that the faith of Christian parents is to be like an heirloom in the family, and the children living within the powerful influence of parental care are to be brought up in "the nurture and admonition of the Lord." They should grow up in love of goodness and remember no definite time when they became "subjects of Christian principle." Here is the genesis of the major thesis that Bushnell was later to propose: "The child is to grow up a Christian and never know himself otherwise."

He sharply criticized what was happening to children within the practices of the church in his day. The prevalent disbelief in the covenant relationship often led parents to "vitiate" the whole spirit and aim of education, and to discourage every effort toward holy virtue in childhood. They were actually taking their children to be aliens, and teaching them that they could do nothing acceptable to God until after their hearts were changed. The result was that children were discouraged and even taught to grow up in sin! Bushnell puts his finger on the dilemma:

> If . . . our view is false, or the current opinion is true, how miserable is the age of childhood! If it may not grow up in holy virtue, if it must grow up in sin, till it comes to some definite age, before it is a candidate for repentance and a new life, then, during that interval, is it seen to lie under a doom more dismal and hapless than any other we are acquainted with in this world. Capable of sin—incapable of repentance! . . . Might not the church better say, in her Savior's name, "Of such is the kingdom of heaven," and clasp it to her arms.[10]

Much of the lack of beauty and maturity in moral character might be traced to this misconception of the Christian religion. For one thing, the person begins to develop a Christian character so late in life that he must maintain "a perpetual and unequal war with previous habit." Christian character needs to be started early, and to grow steadily; it is not "a grape grafted on a bramble." [11]

CAREFUL DISTINCTIONS

It is imperative to note some crucial distinctions made by Bushnell in this early and most significant article. Some writers have intimated that his early theories were largely naturalistic, and that only in his later life, after his earlier optimism and belief in the goodness of man had worn off as a result of the struggles of life, did he really hold to the sinfulness and depravity of man.

Bushnell contends that his view is no infringement upon the doctrine of depravity or the sinfulness of man, but only a more practical remedy to the situation. "It only declares that depravity is best rectified when it is weakest, and before it is stiffened into habit," he affirms.[12]

Another precautionary distinction was his insistence that his views did not infringe upon the doctrine of "spiritual agency," which was operative in bringing persons to a Christian commitment. It is the basis for his later exposition on the "organic unity of the family."

Finally, Bushnell uses the analogy of the mustard seed. The kingdom of heaven, he maintained, is first like a grain of mustard seed, which as it continues to flourish advances toward the stature of a tree. When the Holy Spirit is its root, the church develops its inner life and displays outward activity.

Four months after the publication of his article, Bushnell's health broke. His church decided to send him to Europe for a year and he sailed in July, 1845.

THE BEGINNING OF CONTROVERSY

When Bushnell returned from his trip, he found that his article had raised some dissent in the local ministerial association. He was invited to present his views on Christian education and consequently wrote two sermons, preached them to his congregation, and then read them before the association. The discussion that followed revealed no serious objections to his views. On the contrary, he was requested to print them and they were published under the title *Discourses on Christian Nurture*. His treatise was favorably noticed by an Episcopalian periodical, and it seemed likely to find some favor without causing alarm.

Then there appeared from the North Association of Hartford County, Bennet Tyler's printed pamphlet called *Letter to Dr. Bushnell*. Circulated widely, this tract claimed that the publication *Discourses on Christian Nurture* was full of dangerous tendencies. Visiting a General Association meeting in neighboring Massachusetts, Bushnell suddenly experienced personal and public discourtesies. Soon afterward, the Massachusetts Sabbath School Society suspended publication of his book.

This was sufficient provocation to stir Bushnell. He republished his articles in an 1847 edition entitled *Views of Christian Nurture and of Subjects Adjacent Thereto*. This volume contained the two original "Discourses on Christian Nurture," a rebuttal or set of arguments in defense of the discourses; a reprint of "The Spiritual Economy of Revivals"; an article entitled "Growth, Not Conquest, the True Method of Christian Progress," which was a renaming of his 1844 article "The Kingdom of God as a Grain of Mustard Seed"; a sermon with the title "The Organic Unity of the Family"; and a sermon called "The Scene of the Pentecost and a Christian Parish."

Bushnell had formulated his views of Christian nurture and now was ready to defend them vigorously. He knew his doctrine was in sharp contrast to that of conservative orthodoxy, and a devastating threat to it. He was ready to fight for his position, which was now clearly etched in his mind, encouraged by a wide range of support he had received from those of many denominations.

EXCESSIVE REVIVALISM OPPOSED

Bushnell knew the value and the need of revival but he objected to the fact that revivals had been idolized and at times made the whole of religion. There needed to be more emphasis on Christlike living, less emphasis on preaching or talking, and especially more stress on the nurture of children.

Writing under the stress of controversy, he made some very frank statements in the chapter entitled "Arguments for Discourse in Christian Nurture," which was included in *Views of Christian Nurture*. He said quite bluntly that the more he reflected on the type of religion prevalent in the churches, the more dissatisfied he became. The true test, he believed, is not in the degree of emotional crisis but rather in the quality of love in a person, which manifests itself in the keeping of Christ's commandments. He illustrated convincingly how deceptive is the practice of putting undue importance upon the "emotional" element in a conversion experience. He called for more natural training, gradual habit formation, and much careful thought to accompany the emotions of religion.

It is in his "Argument" that Bushnell also makes explicit his rejection of the ictic theory of God. Bushnell coins this phrase from the Latin word *ictus* meaning "stroke." This was a theory that seemed to be saying that the human race instinctively hates God, that the more it knows of God's character the more it hates him, until a divine stroke or ictus suddenly reverses the instinct so that men love God where they had previously hated him. Everything seemed to depend on this divine stroke, upon this sudden bolt of lightning from on high. Bushnell is ready to replace such a theory with his doctrine of the mediate and immediate influence of God's spirit.

The final exposition of his doctrine was published in the 1861 volume entitled *Christian Nurture*. Thus, through many years and a variety of situations, Bushnell gradually formulated and crystallized his doctrine of nurture. Even in his final volume he adds a few new statements concerning revivalism to the growing list of striking sentences already penned. He maintains that the Christian life is no "camp meeting scene" but must be lived among the tasks and trials of everyday affairs in a practical way.

The far-reaching implications of such thought helped America turn a corner in its spiritual development. One church historian has concluded that Bushnell's volumes on Christian nurture "did perhaps more than any other single agency to break down the extreme individualism of the old Puritan theology of America." [13]

chapter 6 THE CHRISTIAN
NURTURE
OF CHILDREN

In his exposition of Christian nurture Bushnell goes to
the heart of the issue by examining the basic motivation in the
whole process of Christian education. In Ephesians 6:4, the
New Testament writer advised concerning children, "Bring
them up in the nurture and admonition of the Lord." Bushnell
believes that such nurture should derive a quality and power
from the Lord, and should be consistent with his ways, achiev-
ing results far surpassing the effects of mere human method.
He cannot agree with the assumption of many of his neighbors
"that the child is to grow up in sin, to be converted after he
comes to a mature age." [1]

AIM AND EXPECTATION

It is the firm belief of Bushnell that there must be an aim and
expectation in the minds of parents that some good principle
or response may be awakened in the mind of a child. Right
from the beginning the child should be guided to cling to that
which is right and good. Children lead mixed lives just as
adults do, because even Christian persons must still struggle

with sin and evil. From the dawn of life, therefore, the child may be encouraged to resist wrong and evil, and to respond to the good. If the child forms good habits while very young instead of waiting several years until habits of sin are established, there will be a lesser battle between right and wrong. Enmity against God and a desperate struggle are not always an element in the religious experience of children. However, just as the schoolteacher cannot guarantee that every pupil will learn, so the parent cannot conclude with certainty that every child will grow up in Christian piety. The proper aim is nevertheless an essential part of Christian nurture.

An examination of this exposition of Christian nurture reveals that it revolves around the three main factors: the organic unity of the family, the covenant relationship of children, and the family as a means of grace.

THE ORGANIC UNITY OF THE FAMILY

When he uses the term organic unity, Bushnell is really talking about the family as a primary social unit. *Organic* in this usage belongs to his own era and may prove misleading to the present-day reader. He uses it to describe the powerful psychological bonds between the members of a family unit. The effect of these forces is so strong that it is almost as if the members of a family were parts of an organism.

"They are all locked together, in one cause—in common cares, hopes, offices, and duties," writes Bushnell, "for their honor and dishonor, their sustenance, their ambition, all their objects are common." [2] Everything that transpires within the household has more effect upon the children than is often realized.

He asserts in clear perspective the two sides of human life. In some ways people are individuals, each acting from his own will. In other respects they are open to the changing spirit of the groups to which they belong. This whole factor of the group spirit had been seriously overlooked. He says that there is no such thing as a "pure, separate, individual man, living *wholly* within and from himself." [3]

65

The child's moral character is a growing thing. At first he is subject to the moral agency of the parent and only gradually separates into a complete moral agent in himself. In the dependent relationship to parents, the child is open to impressions, both good and bad, including everything he sees and hears. Indeed, the impressions fashion him quite extensively before his powers of reason come into full play. "His character is forming, under a principle, not of choice, but of nurture." [4]

Placed in such close and dependent relations with the parents, the child is subjected to a law of "moral contagion" and becomes involved in the mixed life of good and evil in which the parents are engaged. Therefore children are included in the iniquities of the parents, and also in the promises of God to those parents who faithfully serve him.

THE COVENANT RELATIONSHIP OF CHILDREN

Before he began publication of his writings on Christian nurture, Bushnell had made a study of baptism. He also gave a series of talks to his congregation which resulted in a severe decline in baptisms. Then he discovered that the doctrines of infant baptism and of church membership of children were closely related to his own doctrine of nurture. He soon restored to a place of prominence the Calvinistic doctrine of the covenant relationship of children.

Bushnell claims that the church's practice of infant baptism is a seal of faith of the parent, whereby the child can be accounted as a believer from the beginning. But he quickly emphasizes the "presumptive" nature of baptism and uses the illustration of a wheat seed which presumably contains within itself a thousand generations of wheat, but which because of some fault of cultivation or damage by disease may never reproduce at all. Similarly, the Christian has presumptively the formative power in his character to assist in producing a like faith in his children, though once again some defect or hindrance may prevent him from doing so.

However, God extends the grace whereby he may accomplish his redemptive purposes through the family and the church.

Bushnell goes back to the covenant which God made with Abraham: "I will establish my covenant between me and thee and thy seed after thee in their generations for an everlasting covenant, to be a God unto thee, and to thy seed after thee" (Gen. 17:7). Bushnell interprets this as a family covenant in which God promised to be the God of the children as well as of the fathers.

It appears that Bushnell was considerably helped and influenced by the English writer Richard Baxter, who lived from 1615 to 1691. Apparently Baxter had been a close disciple of John Calvin and an expositor of his doctrines. Baxter had become a Christian without a violent conversion struggle, and this appealed strongly to Bushnell who referred to him as an illustration of Christian nurture and an exponent of the truth that education could be as much a means of grace as preaching.

Bushnell contended that his view on nurture was not new at all but that it rested on foundations soundly orthodox in the previous history of the Christian church. He referred to statements by Justin Martyr, Irenaeus, Tertullian, Origen, the Shepherd of Hermas, Augustine, Calvin, and Richard Baxter, with a short résumé of the developments in New England history in respect to infant baptism. The observance of baptism served to establish the validity of church membership for children.

Speaking as a trained lawyer, he showed how the civil law recognized the child as a full citizen. Actually it seemed a little absurd to call a child a citizen, because he did not vote, bear arms, or pay taxes. Yet he was treated as a full citizen in his potentiality for the future. In comparison, why should the church not be able to accept the child into full membership and attendant privileges by reason of his potentiality within a Christian family?

Views opposite to his own regarding the baptism and church membership of children were sharply criticized by Bushnell who compared them to the practices of a country that takes in new citizens and naturalizes the parents but excludes the children, shutting the latter out to remain in the status of foreigners and aliens.

67

He offered an even stronger appeal:

> It [Christianity] spreads its arms to say, "For God so loved the world," and even declares that publicans and harlots shall flock in, before the captious priests and princes of the day; and yet it has no place, we are told, for children; children are out of the category of grace!
> . . . They are all outside the salvation-fold, hardening there in the storm, till their choosing, refusing, desiring, sinning power is sufficiently unfolded to have a place assigned them within!   Is this Christianity? [5]

THE FAMILY AS A MEANS OF GRACE

The third main factor in Bushnell's Christian nurture of children is the place that the family, and especially the parents, play in the whole scheme.   Interspersed throughout the whole discussion of his major volume are specific suggestions regarding the types of responsibility that parents have in the total scheme of nurture.

Referring to statements by Richard Baxter and to the later writings of Jonathan Edwards, Bushnell picks up the theme that the family is actually used by God as a means of grace in addition to those of the sacraments and the preaching of God's word.   In identifying the family as a means of grace Bushnell was building on his ideas of the mediate influence of the Holy Spirit.   He also added at once that the "life of God" must reign continuously within the parents if they are to be instrumental in infusing new life into their children.   Thus he protects himself against the possibility of his statement being misconstrued to imply a purely humanistic form of character formation.

He was aware that the Christian life is a struggle for adults and children alike.   At an early age children should be prevailed upon to make "an effort to be good, connecting the fact that God desires it and will help them in the endeavor." [6] When the child cares for that which is right with a fixed love, so that it becomes a motivating power in his life, this attitude becomes a worthy foundation for his responsiveness in his mature years.   What is good, therefore, should be made attractive and pleasant to the child and what is wrong should be presented as undesirable. If this godly training is practiced within families, the benefits will be lasting.

Bushnell believed that true Christian nurture would have an important influence not only on the children but also on the parents. They would learn and grow significantly as they endeavored both to teach and to exemplify the Christian faith in this manner. The natural and spontaneous character of their religious faith at home would then probably begin to modify the atmosphere and the worship at church, making it more realistic and natural, less conventional and dry.

chapter 7 BASIC PREMISES

Five major premises underlie Bushnell's theory of the Christian nurture of children.

THE OMNIPRESENCE OF GOD

The first basic premise is the omnipresence of God. This is the underlying idea in Bushnell's whole exposition. It is a most wholesome one and it gives theological substance to the entire doctrine. In 1838 he treated explicitly God's omnipresence, writing in an article that God is both "in" and "with" all things to bring about his purposes. In other words, God's presence is everywhere and the effect of his presence touches all the different orders of creation. His presence is experienced by men so that God might communicate himself to them and make them more in his likeness. This puts man in continuous relationship to God, and in everlasting dependence upon him. These theories are closely akin to twentieth-century theology.

The primary objective of Bushnell's *Christian Nurture* was to describe the manner in which supernatural grace operates in the lives of people, and most especially in the lives of children.

He set out to show that God can work in the lives of children just as well as in the lives of adults, and that God could do this in a way that was appropriate to the capacities of children.[1]

The relationship of the supernatural to the world of nature occupied his thoughts for some twenty-five years. His ideas on this theme were published in 1860 in a large book entitled *Nature and the Supernatural*.[2]

REGENERATION, A PROCESS

A second key factor in the whole theory of Christian nurture is that of regeneration, or the restoration to God.[3] This he viewed as a growing, developing relationship with God. A Christian is one "who has simply *begun* to love what is good," so why should it be "impossible for a child to make such beginnings of love?" [4]

Bushnell insisted that the Christian life is "no vegetable process" or simple evolvement, but a struggle with evil—a fall and a rescue. It is more than a drill of moralities and the adoption of respectable standards. The struggle with good and evil is all connected with the continuous renewal of relationship with God.

Therefore, the Christian life is both a beginning and a becoming, and children within Christian homes may be enrolled as disciples or learners of Christ as well as adults. The initial "putting on of Christ" becomes important when it is consummated by a continuous "putting on." Christian living involves far more than a single, climactic conversion experience. Bushnell insisted that the Christian must be "Christed" through and through. And he was convinced that children could enter into this continuous renewal of relationship with God.

CAPACITY FOR RESPONSE

A third underlying idea is that the child can make a response to God. This is the corollary of Bushnell's other ideas about the influence of the Holy Spirit and the nature of regeneration.

According to his view, children can, and frequently do, make an enthusiastic response to the true and good things of

71

God and do not have to wait, perhaps for years, for such an emotional experience. It is true, they will respond as children, but their very habit and attitude of making a positive response to God can be easily transposed as their capacities mature. Here Bushnell discards the old New England categories of natural ability and moral inability to stress the capacity of adults and children to respect God.

The self only matures gradually and imperceptibly, and this always in relationship with other people. Moreover, through other people, God exercises a "mediate" influence at the same time as his "immediate" influence. Even as the child or the full-grown man is acting responsively to God, he is involved in the psychological bonds of the family, church, and nation.

HUMAN SINFULNESS

A fourth basic idea in the doctrine of Christian nurture concerns depravity. This factor in man is plainly asserted in the Scriptures and is evident in the affairs of men. It is like an infection that can be communicated to the child.

The power of the unconscious, as well as the conscious, can influence the manner in which parents communicate their sins, like the poisons of their fallen state, to their children. By no means, therefore, can children be left merely to "blossom into character." [5]

Not only does Bushnell show how parents communicate their moral infection to the succeeding generation but also he sets forth a real hope and solemn obligation for parents. Through a system of nurture, they can do much in "mitigating the sad legacy of mischief," which they bestow upon their children.

Bushnell qualified the undue stress upon the depravity of man, but he did not discard the doctrine of sin and the involvement of adults and children in it. He stated emphatically that his theory of nurture was not to be confused with the views of those who assumed both the radical goodness of man and that Christian education was concerned only to educe the goodness that was in people.

His was a realistic view of human nature. While recognizing man's sinful nature, he could still see human potentialities and recommend ways of developing them. He believed that through a system of nurture within Christian families, selfishness and evil in a child could be modified while the child's nature was new and pliant and before it was hardened into habit.

Bushnell's plan of nurture for children, who were involved in the human predicament but also included in the covenant relationship with their Christian parents, was not new in the history of the church. But it contrasted sharply with the practice of the church in New England and was a much-needed tonic for the times.

COMMITMENT

A fifth factor within the doctrine of Christian nurture is Bushnell's distinction between childhood and adulthood. Because his *Christian Nurture* is directed toward the training of children only, there is some confusion when adults apply his doctrine indiscriminately. One misinterpretation is that his whole system of Christian education is purely a naturalistic growth, or educational process, and that he has no place for evangelism, commitment, and personal decision.

On the contrary, he believed that very young children can make continuous responses to the things of God. These responses or small commitments are on a childish level and are not expected to be on a par with adult commitment. They are, nevertheless, genuine and preliminary preparations for mature decision. After the child has grown up within Christian nurture and is a member of the church, he must himself assume his responsibilities in the covenant relationship, making an ultimate declaration of faith that confirms all his parents have previously done in his behalf.[6]

chapter 8 REACTION

A storm of controversy greeted Bushnell's *Discourses on Christian Nurture*, published in 1847. The strong public reaction, provoking a varied body of criticism, expressed both approval and disapproval.

THE CHIEF ANTAGONIST

Bennet Tyler led the attack that managed to precipitate a controversy over the merits of Bushnell's work and by so doing brought his doctrine of nurture to the attention of the reading public. Tyler, head of the seminary established in 1834 at East Windsor, opposed the New Haven theology propounded by Nathaniel Taylor. Although Bushnell had studied under Taylor he did not conform to the New Haven theological system.

Bennet Tyler's *Letter to Dr. Bushnell* loudly proclaimed the "dangerous tendencies" of Bushnell's theory of nurture. This caused the Massachusetts Sabbath Society to panic and to suppress its publication of his two addresses. Recognizing that Bushnell's doctrine was capable of dealing a deathblow to all he himself stood for, Tyler fought a defensive and desperate battle using fair tactics and foul. His argumentation epitomizes the old religious extremes Bushnell was trying to correct.

REBUTTALS, REVIEWS, AND CRITICISMS

It was not long before Bushnell published on his own initiative the volume entitled *Views of Christian Nurture and of Subjects Adjacent Thereto.* This contained his original discourses, plus his fiery "Argument," along with other articles. The volume included a heated rebuttal.

Thirteen different periodicals, representing many denominations, reviewed or commented upon his new doctrine between 1847 and 1849. The Unitarians and the liberal Congregationalists were warmly appreciative of his beliefs. Although they did not agree with his ideas about baptism, both the Baptists and the Episcopalians commented favorably on his writings. The latter wanted more emphasis put on the church and its sacraments as a vehicle of grace, rather than on Bushnell's stress on the family.

Many periodicals praised his criticism of the necessity for a violent conversion experience, his emphasis on the family, and his insight into the psychological bonds of experience. Most of them, however, were disturbed by his tendency toward naturalism and were not happy about his doctrine of man and the manner in which God's grace was supposed to operate in man.

The Christian Observatory (1847) was the most complete in its rejection and denunciation of Bushnell's theory. It even had the effrontery to claim that he was dishonest in advertising that the ministerial association had asked for the publication of his first two discourses.

It was Charles Hodge, writing in the 1847 volume of the *Princeton Review,* who made the most reasoned and serious charges against the naturalism in Bushnell's writings. Hodge claimed that Bushnell's doctrine was based on a false assumption about human nature; namely, that human or parental education can correct its natural corruption.

WORDS OF SUPPORT

Another important review was that of Noah Porter in the 1848 volume of *The New Englander.* He was the son-in-law of Nathaniel Taylor, a constant supporter of the New Haven theology, who later became president of Yale College. His review was unique in that he was in full sympathy with Bushnell's theories and he reprimanded the Massachusetts Sabbath Society for its inappropriate treatment of Bushnell.

In his interesting discussion, Porter suggested that in order to accept the Christian gospel a person did not have to accept a complete system of truth fully adapted and suited to the most reflective mind. This was a refreshing change of outlook, a contrast to the earlier views of ministers and revival leaders in New England. He made another incisive point—one Bushnell elaborated in later writings—that the whole of life is by structure and design a redemptive system under God.

WEAPONS OF CONTROVERSY

The reaction to his early writings both encouraged and angered Bushnell. Much of the criticism touched on weaknesses and lack of clarity in his theory, which later helped in the solidifying and clarifying of his famous doctrine.

In the publication of his "Argument" he gave vent to his ire by berating the Massachusetts Sabbath Society for suddenly suppressing his book without any word of explanation either to himself or the public:

> The "Letter" is a remarkably quiet epistle, but it has been very industriously circulated and the "dangerous tendencies," like the fuse hissing upon a bomb, have thrown the ancient and honorable commonwealth of Massachusetts, including, for aught that appears, the Ancient and Honorable Artillery Company itself, into a general panic.[1]

Although he wrote with a good deal of indignation, he began in this article to grapple with the charges of naturalism and included in it several new statements about Christian nurture. During this controversial period his thought processes were stimulated in many ways for the writing of his 1861 volume, *Christian Nurture.*

RESISTING CHARGES OF NATURALISM

Bushnell was aware that his whole doctrine would have been accepted more readily had he based it solely upon the covenant relationship. But he deliberately couched his language in more naturalistic forms, showing how God exerts his supernatural grace through natural media to influence and to win the response of man. Here was a departure from a substantial view in which God had miraculously to insert a new germ, almost a new substance, into a person before he could begin to be a Christian. Bushnell introduced the "influence" that occurs in personal relationships as more appropriate to describe the relationship between a man and a personal God.

A second edition of *Views of Christian Nurture* was published in 1848 and ten years later there appeared a comprehensive volume entitled *Nature and the Supernatural as Together Constituting the One System of God*. In the former he made a succinct statement in a two-page footnote concerning the relationship of the natural and the supernatural, and in the latter he gave an extensive treatment of the topic with which he had wrestled for many years.

In 1861 he published his final volume on *Christian Nurture*, nearly fourteen years after the publication of his original *Discourses on Christian Nurture*. It was a more mature and quietly reasoned statement, expanded to remedy some of the earlier criticisms. By then, time had removed the bitterness from the controversy over the doctrine of nurture. Bushnell had struggled to produce, within the severities of New England theology, a new doctrine concerning the religious life of children; his theory had been tempered in the ensuing reaction and controversy; and finally he had submitted his ideas in an elaborated form, which was to prove a classic text in Christian education.

PART III   PROVOCATIVE THEOLOGIAN

chapter 9   INGENIOUS
THINKER,
PROVOCATIVE
AND
UNSYSTEMATIC

In the preface to his *Views of Christian Nurture,* Bushnell points out that the question of Christian nurture is one which involves "all the most abstruse points in theology." [1] His educational theory had much practical sense and many strong convictions. As a preacher his practical interests made him more concerned about throwing light on the issues of life than in developing a system of theology.

It is not easy to summarize Bushnell's writings, for he was far from being a systematic writer. His whole life and work was a reaction against the formal, logical systematization of the New England theologians before him. He was more interested in "expression" than "definition." His very theory of language and mode of writing made him radically different from his contemporaries. He concluded at times with an inadequate statement of theology, or he entangled himself in contradictory sayings. Often he altered and modified his views from one book to another.

Bushnell approached religion from an experiential viewpoint. His own personal religious experience led him into independent thoughts about God. From his college days he had become convinced that religion must be of the heart as well as of the mind. Religion for him was more practical, warm, and uplifting than the massive deliberations of the customary theological treatises.

Primarily a preacher, he expressed his perceptions most clearly in his sermons, observing lives of people and preaching the gospel to them in a personal and firsthand manner. The difficulty came when he tried to use this knowledge for the purpose of formal disquisitions. As Bushnell tried to defend himself from keen-eyed critics, he frequently was forced back into the very method of theologizing against which he had been reacting.

> "New light" was always coming to him. He cared more for the new than the old, nor was he careful to preserve a formal harmony between them. More than once he virtually retracted or greatly altered positions he had taken, but, it should be said, generally not with advantage to himself as a thinker. His first contentions usually carried his real convictions, and he gravitated back to them.[2]

Almost simultaneously he received invitations to deliver graduation addresses at the Divinity School in Cambridge, which was Unitarian; at the Theological Seminary in Andover, which strongly opposed Unitarianism; and at the Divinity School in New Haven. Fired with a new spiritual elevation and religious intensity, he delivered three different addresses, later published in the volume *God in Christ*,[3] all based on the text of 1 John 1:2 which had become so meaningful to him.

In delivering these addresses under the power of his new religious experience, he endeavored not only to be a mediator between the Congregationalists and the Unitarians, but also he launched into a discussion of the doctrines of the Trinity, Christology, and the Atonement—orthodox statements that had long troubled him. This was no small thing for a preacher to undertake in the presence of faculty and students of three theological schools! Inspired by courage and enthusiasm he made some excellent points, but he also made some rash statements and some unfortunate pronouncements.

Bushnell wrote first and studied later. This was as true of his theological writing as it was of his exposition of the theory of nurture. After his lectures at the divinity schools appeared in print, heated controversy began which sometimes gave rise to charges of heresy. In order to defend and elaborate his views he published *Christ in Theology*,[4] a book that showed the evidence of much reading but also illustrated his weakness of writing without sufficient preparation.

Theodore T. Munger, a biographer of Bushnell, gives an accurate and concise evaluation in words difficult to surpass:

> All through, in his writings and his life, he forces upon us the conclusion that there were a few general truths which he held half intuitively and wholly by reflection, from which he never substantially departed. His mind was of the intuitive order, and his strength lay there. He is best seen and most fairly judged by his simple and large contentions, and not by his refinements upon them. These primitive, spontaneous assertions made him a modern man; his explanations put him back among those spinners of theology whose company he had forsaken at the outset; try as he might, he could not make himself at home among them. . . . What he felt he trusted, and what he saw he knew. When he speculated he became uncertain, and finally gravitated back to his first positions.[5]

It should be noted that Bushnell did not originate his theological ideas in a vacuum. He had been influenced by several writers, among them Samuel Taylor Coleridge, who wrote *Aids to Reflection*. This work had a profound impact upon Bushnell's theory of language and his understanding of God's relationship to the world of nature.

Bushnell also had read Moses Stuart's translation of Schleiermacher's critique of Sabellius and discovered the ideas presented there to be similar to his own. He was acquainted with the writings of Neander, a Jew converted to Christianity by Schleiermacher, and quoted him occasionally.

There were many powerful forces at work in New England at the time: the advance of science and the new textual criticism; Unitarian rationalism and the writings of Theodore Parker; transcendentalism and the writings of Ralph Waldo Emerson; the clamor of new social classes for eloquent speakers; a pervading empiricism and a new American nationalism.[6] It was in this intellectual and social flux that Bushnell attempted to work out his new statements of theology—a theology that attempted to present an interpretation of the Christian faith that was relevant to the ferment of the times.

chapter 10   DOCTRINE
OF   GOD

Bushnell stated his ideas about the majesty and transcendence of God most strikingly in his 1848 address to the Yale Divinity School, which was later reprinted in God in Christ.[1]

He began his address by asserting that "God exceeds our measure, and must, until either he becomes less than infinite or we more than finite." [2]   He also stated that "God unrevealed is God simply existing, as spirit, in himself." [3]   Bushnell refused to anthropomorphize God, and realized that God could not have form, space, or motion, like objects in the temporal world. He explained further:

> Observe that, when God is revealed it cannot be as the One, as the Infinite, or Absolute, but only as through media.   And as there are no infinite media, no signs that express the infinite, no minds, in fact, that can apprehend the infinite by direct inspection, the One must appear in the manifold; the Absolute in the conditional; Spirit in form; the Motionless in motion; the Infinite in the finite.   He must distribute himself; he must let forth his nature in sounds, colors, forms, works, definite objects, and signs.[4]

GOD'S CAPACITY FOR SELF-EXPRESSION

God, then, has a totally unique capacity for producing himself in finite forms, for generating a knowledge of himself in man.[5] This unique capacity underlies all revelation, and only through revelation can man know God:

> There is in God, taken as the Absolute Being, a capacity of self-expression, so to speak, which is peculiar — a generative power of form, a creative imagination, in which, or by aid of which, he can produce himself outwardly, or represent himself in the finite. In this respect, God is wholly unlike to us.[6]

Bushnell understood the creation of the world or worlds as the first revelation of God. He identified the Logos, the Word, as the "Form of God." The second great revelation is that of the incarnation in which God revealed himself in human form through Jesus Christ.

After the coming of Christ, men and the Scriptures began to speak of the Father, Son, and Holy Spirit. Bushnell interpreted these three concepts as the necessary manifestations of an absolute God in the complex task of revealing himself to man. The mystery and the paradox of the three persons and the one God were part of the mysterious fact of the infinite God becoming finite. He wrote:

> I do not undertake to fathom the interior being of God, and tell how it is composed. . . . I only insist that, assuming the strictest unity and even simplicity of God's nature, he could not be efficiently or sufficiently revealed to us, without evolving a trinity of persons, such as we meet in the Scriptures. These persons or personalities are the *dramatis personae* of revelation, and their reality is measured by what of the infinite they convey in these finite forms. As such they bear, on the one hand, a relation to God, who is to be conveyed, or imported into knowledge; on the other, they are related to our human capacities and wants, being that presentation of God

which is necessary to make him a subject of thought, or bring him within the discourse of reason; that also which is necessary to produce mutuality, or terms of conversableness, between us and him, and pour his love most effectually into our feeling.[7]

Bushnell claimed that man could never penetrate into the inscrutable mystery of God's inner being and that other writers have been presumptuous in their pronouncements. He believed the mystery of the Trinity should be received "under the simple conditions of expression" and that no attempt to fit it into the exact categories of science or logic could succeed.

A SUPERNATURAL GOD AND HIS NATURAL WORLD

Bushnell had long opposed and resented the New England theology, which made a sharp duality between the things of God and the things of the world, and which made any action of God upon a human life a "bolt from the blue" that had no connection with everyday life. He explained that God could work through the natural laws of the world as truly as he could work in a sudden inrush and display of power upon a human soul. He portrayed God as acting in the common events of life as well as in the great drama of redemption. This did not mean that he had dispensed with the supernatural and the transcendent.

He maintained that the natural and the supernatural are two utterly distinct realms, differing both in kind and in function. In his thought, nature is that realm of being or substance within the space-time world which operates according to inherent laws of cause and effect. The supernatural is characterized by freedom and is not in the chain of natural cause and effect, but rather acts upon the natural chain of cause and effect from without. There is a direct antithesis between the two, yet they act and react upon each other so that *together* they make "the true system of God," which is something greater than the universe we know.[8]

He tried to distinguish the two corresponding classes of being as "things" and "powers." "Things" he conceived as being mechanically under law from the very beginning; they act only in the way that their law determines; they remain in the form in which they are made.[9] "Powers" he defined as follows:

> All free intelligences, . . . the created and the uncreated, are, as being free, essentially supernatural in their action; having all, in the matter of their will, a power transcending cause and effect in nature, by which they are able to act on the lines and vary the combinations of natural causalities. . . . They are powers, not things; the radical idea of a power being that of an agent, or force, which acts from itself, uncaused; initiating trains of effect that flow from it.[10]

Because of man's freedom and ability to manipulate the things of nature, Bushnell classified man as a supernatural "power." And God, as the "uncreated Power at the head of his immense family of powers" became the "major term of all existence." [11]

In the view of Bushnell, both man and God act upon the natural world, not in a way which overturns nature and subverts its laws, but in the normal way in which supernatural powers work upon the world of things. God's real kingdom is a kingdom of powers and he the "Regal Power."

Bushnell believed that God is a "living God," and that he is just as active in the present as he was at the beginning of creation—and that he will remain so for eternity. Therefore, God can and does employ the world of things to deal with the needs of his children.[12] Nature, as the domain of cause and effect, is "only the *platform* on which he establishes his kingdom as a kingdom of minds, and persons." [13] In another place, referring to men and God as "powers" in relationship to nature as a "thing," he wrote, "Both he and they are continually using the Thing and pouring their activity into it, as the *medial point of their relationship*." [14] He rapped the "shallow pride" and the "idolatry of science" which the growing naturalism of the late 1850's was employing in its enthusiasm over the natural world. He felt that the topic of creation was beyond the exercises of philosophy.

In the early part of his *Nature and the Supernatural*, Bushnell plainly stated that the genuine supernaturalism of Christianity signified a God working beyond the lines of cause and effect to remedy a disordered humanity in a way that would never occur according to natural laws. He claimed that the world itself has been "unmade" by sin and turned into a "state of unnature." [15] Thus for Bushnell, the natural world cannot be classified as God's sole and proper system because it needs an intervention and supernatural remedy from without. Nature is instrumental and complemental to a larger system of God.[16] In this larger system, the kingdom of God is a "Supernatural dispensatory of healing and salvation for the race," and Christianity is a "historically supernatural movement on the world" instituted by Jesus Christ.[17]

THE PERSONAL CHARACTER OF GOD

In his volume entitled *Christ in Theology*, Bushnell discussed the personal character of God. Contemplation of the absolute God, he felt, tends to obscure the personal element in God. He attributed this tendency to the difficult process whereby men try to form a conception of God. First, they impute to God certain elements found in their own personal lives, and then, to save God's infinity, deny them again. In the struggle to conceive of God by this positive and then negative process, in the attempt to subtract human qualities in order to grasp infinite qualities, their understanding of the personal nature of God often suffers. This latter quality Bushnell wished to maintain. He felt the doctrine of the Trinity was helpful because it "holds us to a strain of thought after God, both as *transcending* the categories of human understanding and as *personal* in his relations and character." [18]

It was Bushnell's contention that because of the living, personal relation between God and man, the formulas of logic from the mechanical, natural world were quite inadequate. He believed that this was the defect at the base of much theological thinking and he sought to correct it with his new theory of language.

As Bushnell discussed God's operation within the world of nature, he implicitly retained the personal character of God in respect to all his dealings with men. In describing the way God used society for training his children in *Nature and the Supernatural*, he wrote that "meantime God is reigning over it, socially relating himself to each member, governing and training that member through his own liberty." [19]

This is reminiscent of Bushnell's doctrine of God's omnipresence, examined earlier, which presented God's "Spirit" as interchangeable with God's "Presence," establishing a fixed relationship between God's mediate and immediate agency in human lives. Bushnell was firmly convinced that God uses parents, teachers, neighbors, and other persons as "media" through which he exerts his influence and power.

Though God uses nature in many ways, it seemed obvious to Bushnell that the simple operations of nature did not minister to man's rebellious spirit, to the cries of his repentance, or to his struggles of faith. God's supernatural providence toward persons was "more warmly reciprocal" than in his general providence within the natural world. Nature was viewed as a constant quantity that God uses in his relationship with man, even though God is not confined within it. Bushnell summarized his thinking with this statement:

By means of the constant element between us and God —limbered, though constant, to our common action— we are set in terms of *reciprocity* as living persons or powers, and are found acting toward each other in a perpetual *dialogue* of parts. Taken thus, in the whole comprehension of its import, our world is nothing but a vast, special, supernatural, reciprocal Providence, in which our God is reigning as an ever-present, ever-mindful *counselor, and guide, and friend*, a redeemer of our sin, a hearer of our prayers.[20]

Bushnell's strong statement about the relationship of God to man within the framework of personal dialogue and reciprocity shows clearly that he was far ahead of his time.

GOD'S RIGHTEOUSNESS EMPHASIZED

The righteousness of God was another dominant theme in the mind of Bushnell. Other writers had characterized God's sovereignty as arbitrary and unpredictable. For Bushnell this was unthinkable. His compulsion to maintain the righteousness of God, linked together with his preoccupation with the topic of law, led him to introduce an incompatible element into his doctrine of God. This was another outcropping of the basic paradox within him.

Since nature and human nature were so closely governed by law, he thought that God would also operate by a strict system of law. At this point he forgot his earlier cautions about predicating things of human life to God. Bushnell argued that because God's purpose never varies and his reason is perfect, his supernatural workings are by immutable, universal, and fixed laws. He likened God to an omniscient chess player who, in any given set of circumstances, knows the right move to make; and if he plays the game a million times, given the same circumstances, he will always make the same move. In saying that God would always work toward a "law of one's own end" as a morally perfect being, he failed to realize that God's perfection removes the idea of obligation, and that in God the "ought" and the "is" are identical.

Bushnell's aim to show the dependability and righteousness of God was commendable, but he went too far in looking for law in God. At one point he posited a "law of right" which he held to be in existence even before God! [21] Bushnell's emphasis on law served to balance his mystical tendencies with realism as he spoke about character and righteousness in men, but when he began to incorporate this emphasis into speculations about God and his origins it became a detracting factor.

In his book entitled *Vicarious Sacrifice* he projected the implications of the "law of love" for the atonement. He began with the idea that love is a principle essentially vicarious in its own nature. Given the universality of the law of love, the universality of vicarious sacrifice is also given. Christ's sacrifice on the cross was therefore nothing strange but only the fulfillment of his obligation under love. If the principle of vicarious suffering was binding upon Christ, then it was eternally binding upon God. In direct contrast to many of his colleagues who held to the "impassibility" of God, Bushnell dealt frequently with the thought that God was involved in suffering love for his children.

Bushnell's basic idea of God's deep involvement in the atonement was commendable, and an improvement on the atonement theology of New England orthodoxy. The defect and weakness in his thinking was the manner in which he arrived at the idea. He saw God and all moral natures as obligated to the law of right and the law of love.[22] Bushnell put altogether too much "obligation" upon God. He would have done well to have reversed the direction of his reasoning and to have interpreted the implications and obligations of God's revelation for men. Speaking of God as a chess player and emphasizing how he followed law and order, Bushnell neglected to spell out in adequate terms the dealings of a personal God with personal beings who very often chose to be disobedient, illogical, and unlawful. The realm of love and personal relationships greatly transcend the connotations that go with law.

For his time, Bushnell achieved many valuable and provocative insights concerning God. But having achieved a fresh insight into the personal relationship between God and man, he failed to spell out fully the true implications of it. Instead, he reverted to his old preoccupation with law, which obscured his new theories and involved him in serious difficulties. Although he had crossed new frontiers he was not able to work his intuitive findings into a fully consistent system of theology.

chapter 11 DOCTRINE OF MAN

The essential nature of man, according to Bushnell, is his dependence upon God. By nature man is a personal being whose very existence and wholeness depends on his relationship with God. This conviction Bushnell stressed most clearly in his sermons. Man is "a being made for God and religion" who both needs and wants God "just as a child's nature wants a mother and father." [1] This need is not always conscious, but without God life is abortive.

MAN'S DISTINCTIVE CHARACTERISTICS

The uniqueness of man in contrast to all other beings is his capacity to receive the intimations and inspirations of God. Because of this capacity, man can perceive intuitive truths. "Man is designed, in his very nature," said Bushnell, "to be a partially mystic being; the world to be looked upon as a mystic world." [2]

In his treatise *Nature and the Supernatural*,[3] which was completed in 1858 and published in 1860, he dealt extensively with the doctrine of man. This volume was issued before his final volume about Christian nurture appeared. Hence, these ideas were thoroughly developed during the final preparations of the nurture classic.

In his treatise he classed man as a supernatural "power" with freedom and self-will as contrasted to "things," which in Bushnell's thought are always subject to the law of cause and effect in the natural world.[4] Powers, acting in liberty, are capable of a double action—to do, or not to do; things can only act in the way their law determines. Powers are perfectible through exercise; things are perfect as made. Powers are perfected only by a schooling of their own consent; things are under mechanical law alone. Powers can violate a present harmony and introduce disorder into it; things are incapable of disorder unless affected by malign action from without.[5] Man thus has the distinction of being a finite "power," able to act upon nature from without the law of cause and effect in a manner similar to that of God, the infinite Power.

MORAL RESPONSIBILITY

In developing his doctrine of man, Bushnell pointed out that man has the unusual gift of self-determining will and knows consciously that he is responsible and accountable to God for the responses he makes to God.

Bushnell was aware that man cannot always carry out the choices he makes. Though he is sovereign in his self-determination, though he is a supernatural "power" unconfined to the causality of nature, he is nevertheless conditioned and influenced by such causality. He lives in nature; he is environed by nature; he acts through nature. Certain parts of his makeup—such as his appetite, memory, and disposition—are affected by laws of cause and effect. His faculties are partly governed by natural laws and partly subject to his governing will. Man's "executive capacity" is subject to physiological and cerebral limitations, conditions of want, ignorance, prejudice, superstition, habits, and passions.[6]

Yet, in Bushnell's system of "powers" with free moral choice, there is inherent a possibility of the wrong choice as well as the right choice. Part of God's plan seems to be "to establish his powers in the right, by allowing them an experiment of the wrong, in which to school their liberty." Then, by a de-

91

livering process, God brings them up out of the bitterness of this experiment, so that with an intelligent and permanent abhorrence of the wrong, they make a glad and free response to the good, and to God.[7]

WHY IS THERE SIN?

But Bushnell was troubled by the presence of sin and its relationship to life itself. He devoted an entire chapter to the problem.[8] If there is a training and discipline in liberty, why must man always break away from God and fall into sin? Bushnell was certain that God does not will or desire it, and that when it takes place it is "against his will and against every attribute of his infinitely beneficent and pure character."[9] He thought of sin as an incident-peril in the creation of moral and accountable beings—a peril which God certainly does not desire.

Man is subject, as a "power," to the moral law, wherein to know the right is to be under obligation to it. But there is an empirical side to life. Through his experience of "seeing, doing, suffering, comparing, distinguishing, and other like operations," man builds the "furniture" of his character. A thing in nature is under fixed laws of causation from the beginning. "But free agents are weak because they are free," wrote Bushnell, "left to act originatively, held fast by no superior determination, bound to no sure destiny; save as they are trained into character, in and through [this] *experience*."[10]

While Bushnell had drastically altered the New England associationist psychology of his day by insisting on man's unique capacity for self-determination, he recognized that there remains an empirical element that affects man's will.

Bushnell believed that man is morally responsible and guilty if he makes the wrong choice. His curiosity about the mystery of evil lures man into breaking off an excellent and loving relationship with God. Though he does not know beforehand the implications of wrong choices, he does know consciously beforehand the wrongness of his choices and is, therefore, morally responsible. Bushnell flatly rejected the claims of the increasingly popular naturalistic philosophers who reduced all human wrong to weakness, thereby obliterating any distinction between good and evil.[11]

The freshness of Bushnell's ideas may be better understood when it is remembered that he was rejecting the new naturalism and also reacting violently against the doctrinaire New England theology. The latter had deduced that God in his omnipotence and sovereignty, for some inscrutable reason, wants sin and misery in his creation as part of his ideal plan! [12]

Bushnell pointed out that even the knowledge which comes from sin may be of value in God's redemptive activity. The helplessness, despair, and sense of disability resulting from such knowledge prepares the possibility in man of a new creation. "Impotence discovered is the capacity of redemption," he wrote. When a soul is restored to God and truly regenerated by him, then his "bad experience" can be the condition of its everlasting stability and strength.[13]

Bushnell's thinking was always imprinted with the pattern from the mold of his own experience—a mold of religious development from the legal to a personal relationship with God. He failed to perceive that a person does not need to undergo, in strict historical time sequence, first the Old Testament relationship and then the New Testament relationship. In his preoccupation with law, in his identification of the law of right with God, he obscured and lost some of the beauty and glory of the relationship with a personal God. In this argument, at least, he failed to see that a person, though still enmeshed in the sins of finite and perverse human nature, could respond to God because of the grace and personal relationship first offered him by God.

MAN'S NEED OF REGENERATION

In his sermons Bushnell showed a profound comprehension of the personal quality of man's sin against God. Dealing with man's unique power, he said: "How sublime a creature must that be, call him either man or demon, who is able to confront the Almighty and tear himself away from his throne!" [14] In another sermon he commented on what a "falling short" it is

93

when men fall short of God. In their self-centeredness "they tear themselves away" from God with devastating results.[15] Elsewhere, he indicated that sin plays havoc with the very "image of God" in which man has been created, and makes his soul "a truly deformed creature." [16]

Bushnell thoroughly rejected the liberal concepts of sin which were becoming popular. He stoutly resisted all pantheistic naturalism that would make God into "a tardy but sublime Naturus," and would pardon men of sin by calling it "development." Such development excuses men "because [they] are only parts of nature subject to her laws; parts, that is, of God, and subject to the eternal fate that rules him." [17]

He deliberately set out to refute the notion that development was a universal panacea for all the evils of the world.[18] He claimed that man could not remedy his disorders and sin by self-originated and self-cultivated virtue, thereby dispensing with any supernatural aids.[19] He kept insisting that the "supernatural interference" and the regeneration process must come from God.[20] He believed that man's sin and wrong choices have spoiled the pure spontaneity and the right use of his unique liberty. The harmony of his soul has been broken, his loving and obedient responses to God have been mutilated by his perversities. Man must have the "ingeneration of God," a full and refreshing inspiration from God, a new birth of God's spirit within him to restore him to the exercise of his true liberty as a son.[21] Bushnell ended his argument with these words:

> There is, then, we conclude, no hope of a restoration of society, or of a religious upraising of man, except in a supernatural and divine operation. Progress under sin, by laws of natural development, is a fiction—there is no hope of progress, apart from the regenerative and quickening power of a grace that transcends mere natural conditions and causes.[22]

Bushnell rejected Emerson's views on man and contended that "grazing in the field of nature is not enough for a being whose deepest affinities lay hold of the supernatural, and reach after God." [23]

Earlier in his career, Bushnell had been more optimistic and naïve concerning man and his progress in the world. In 1843 he delivered an address to the Society of Alumni of Yale College entitled "The Discourse on the Moral Tendencies and Results of Human History." [24] He was a minister at that time and he spoke with considerable eloquence and enthusiasm.

He believed there would come a day when the "dominion of ignorance and physical force" would cease to rule the world; when "beauty, reason, science, personal worth, and religion" would come into their rightful supremacy; when "liberty and equality" would be so established that every man would have the right to his existence and to an honorable, happy one; when war would be abolished "by the progress of liberty and intelligence." [25]

He urged his hearers, as scholars, to "have faith in the future." He pointed out that "power moves in the direction of hope," and indeed, hope was one of the persistent qualities he expressed throughout his life. Eloquent about the greatness of American life, he advised that "everything true, just, pure, good, great," could here unfold itself without hindrance. But even in the midst of this much-criticized address he made this interesting statement: "Consider *how God has stood by man's history* and labored with him in his crudest follies, and even by means of them continued to help him on." [26] Man did not progress by his own powers alone.

Bushnell's doctrine of man, then, had many strong points and some weak ones. His preoccupation with law resulted in much inconsistency and weakness. He was, however, enough of a rebel not to follow either orthodox Calvinism or the rising naturalism of his day. His independent and creative thinking was a healthy influence, even though he did not develop it into a thoroughly systematic theology.

chapter 12 DOCTRINE
OF CHRIST

The most serious defects of Bushnell's theology are revealed in
his doctrine of Christ. Here he demonstrated most painfully
his inadequacy as a systematic theologian. In 1848, after his
own personal vision of God, he addressed the Yale College
Commencement on "The Divinity of Christ." [1]   At this time
he was enthusiastic about the direct revelation of God, but he
lacked a knowledge of church history and his exuberance led
to unfortunate extremes. His Christology, or doctrine of the
person of Christ, suffered the most objections.

THE PERSON OF CHRIST
Bushnell began with the claim that Christ was divine and that
he was different from other men not in degree, but in kind.
As God manifested, the least known facet of his nature was the
human. To support a superhuman understanding of Jesus he
cataloged ten proofs. These included such things as the pre-
existence, miraculous birth, the fact of the incarnation or Word
made flesh, and the significance of scripture passages such as
"In him dwelleth all the fullness of the Godhead bodily." He
added that if Jesus were not superhuman he displayed great

audacity in referring to his relationship to God in such words
as, "He that hath seen me hath seen the Father." If Jesus
were not superhuman there could be no greater effrontery conceived than his statement, "No man cometh unto the Father,
but by me." It was no ordinary human being who was gravely
telling the world, "My Father is greater than I." Moreover, his
uniqueness was signified by the inclusion of the Son in the bap-
tismal formula of "Father, Son, and Holy Ghost." [2]

Another point that led Bushnell to his unbalanced view
was the sinlessness of Jesus. He said that "if the man Jesus
never makes the experiment of sin, it must be because the divine is so far uppermost in him as to suspend the proper man-
hood of his person." [3]

In his christological evaluations, Bushnell repeatedly dis-
counted the humanity of Jesus Christ. By "proving" the divinity of Christ he did a great injustice to the human element
in Jesus, which theologians throughout Christian history have
struggled to maintain. Bushnell concluded with an outright
statement of the "impersonal humanity" of Jesus Christ. He
stated that Jesus was "scarcely more than a mere nominal man,"
with the divine so predominant in him that he did not even
"unfold a human character." [4] "We have a man without a
man," he added.[5] Bushnell would even question the reality
of Jesus' physical development as well as whether his growth
was that of an ordinary child. God could manifest himself in
the ways of a child as well as in the ways of the world, or of
a man. He believed God could "act" a human person without being measured by so doing, just as he could shine through
the finite creation of the world without being measured by it.[6]
The extremity of Bushnell's thought is reflected in his words,
"Even to say that Christ reasons and thinks, using the words in
their human sense, is quite as repugnant to his proper deity, as
to say that he learns or grows in knowledge." [7] To add to
the argument, Bushnell pointed out that the Scriptures did
not say that the human soul called Jesus had obeyed and suffered, but rather, "he who was in the form of God, humbled
himself and became obedient unto death, even the death of

the cross." [8] Moreover, Jesus Christ had prayed, "O Father, glorify thou me with thine own self, with the glory which I had with thee before the world was"—a prayer that could not come from a human soul even if he had possessed one.

In the volume *Nature and the Supernatural*, Bushnell later used these christological ideas as the basis for a chapter on the life, manner, and teachings of Jesus. The chapter was written in a somewhat romantic vein and glowed with enthusiasm about the ideal life of Jesus. In another chapter entitled "The Character of Jesus Forbids His Possible Classification with Men," [9] Bushnell was intrigued with what he called the "passive side" of Jesus' character. He pointed out that it was the general impression among people that "patience, gentleness, readiness to suffer wrong without resistance" were signs of weakness.[10]

> But Christ, in opposition to all such impressions, manages to connect these nonresisting and gentle passivities with a character of the severest grandeur and majesty; and, what is more, convince us that no truly great character can exist without them.[11]

It is difficult to understand why Bushnell should classify these elements of strong character as "passive," for it did an injustice to the conception of Jesus Christ himself, and especially to his atoning work.

THE INCARNATION

Bushnell had a profound sense of the reality and significance of the incarnation as a fact in the scheme of world history. In 1848 he stated that the representation and expression of the infinite God in a finite human person was as magnificent as the creation of the world itself. It amounted to an "incorporation of the Divine in the history of the world—so a renovation, at last, of the moral and religious life of the world." [12]

In the 1858 treatise, *Nature and the Supernatural*, he stated that there was "no hope of a restoration of society, or of a religious upraising of man, except in a supernatural and divine

operation." [13]   This has already taken place in the "bodying
out" of God in his form or Logos, into the human Jesus Christ.
Bushnell saw Christianity as a "historically supernatural movement on the world" that was brought into existence and or-
ganized by the person of Jesus Christ. "He therefore is the
central figure and power, and with him the entire fabric either
stands or falls." [14]

THE ATONING WORK OF CHRIST

Bushnell's theories about the atoning work of Christ were
a radical departure from the orthodox theology of his contemporaries. New England had become absorbed in a ponderous
system of morality. Following the new ideas of Jonathan Edwards, atonement was believed to apply not only to a few elect,
but to all people. It was, however, given a legalistic twist, in
that the atonement was thought to set right and to maintain
God's government of justice in the universe. This view was
called the "governmental theory of the atonement." By "ex-
pressing" God's hatred of sin, the general justice of God had
been sustained so that God was able to forgive sin.

Bushnell believed the effect of the atonement was not to
help a person escape the wrath of God, or to get to heaven, or
to be counted among the elect. Rather, the end and purpose
of Christ's atoning work was "to renovate character, to quicken
by the infusion of new life." [15] His insight that the Christian
life involves a transformation of character helped him immeas-
urably in all his doctrines.

Another orthodox view regarded the death of Christ as an
"expression of abhorrence to sin, made through the suffering of
one, in place of the same expression that was to be made, by
the suffering of many." [16] Such abhorrence indicated that God
had maintained justice and therefore was free to forgive without jeopardizing the structure of the universe. Bushnell had
many reasons why he could not accept such theories of atonement. For example, he did not believe that a good God would
impose his displeasure and abhorrence upon the innocence of
Christ; and if Christ were God and one of the three Persons of

the Trinity, then such penal distribution was going on wholly within God himself, and all others were spectators.[17]

He also mentioned that Christ had manifested this "Eternal Life" in an evil history, in the midst of an "alienated, averted race." [18] By bringing the divine into human history and setting up the kingdom of heaven, Christ had broken the authority of social evil. He also embodied the movement of the divine upon the individual that cleared away the disabilities caused by sin in man's nature and that saved man from the internal bondage of evil.[19]

In attempting to free himself from the undesirable aspects of penal or substitutionary theories of the atonement of Christ, Bushnell moved to a moral view of atonement. His concern was to stress what the life and death of Christ *expresses*. God's character, power, and eternal life were expressed in visible form and within social relationships in the life of Christ. The very life of God had been expressed in Christ as a power to regenerate and quicken human character. Bushnell also stressed that the atoning mission of Christ was addressed to the feeling or sensibility of man. Logic and dogmatic formulas could not encompass the manner in which God expresses himself.[20]

Looking upon the trial, the persecution, the crucifixion, the death of Christ upon the cross, Bushnell asked: "What man of our race beholding this strange history of the Word, will not feel a new courage enter into his soul?" [21] Men dare to hope again. They find God close to them in such a way as to inspire courage. God is not the implacable avenger, which their guilty fears had supposed, but rather a friend, a God of love. And so Bushnell revealed the essence of his moral view of atonement in these words:

> They have a feeling of something like justification, even
> if they have never heard of it—a feeling, which if it
> were to vent itself in language, would say, Therefore
> we are freely justified by grace. It is not that the suffer-
> ing appeases God, but that it expresses God—displays,
> in open history, the unconquerable love of God's heart.[22]

Unfortunately, as soon as he had introduced this radical new approach for understanding the atonement, he reverted to his old theme song about "law," stating that the suffering of Christ reconsecrated the desecrated law of God.

In the description of the suffering and death of Christ in *God in Christ*, Bushnell mentioned the "patience of his trial, the meekness of his submission to injustice, and the malignant passions of his enemies." [23] Later he referred to Christ's "attitude of submission to evil," and to his "meekness of love." [24] For some reason, Bushnell incorporated this "passive" quality into his concept of Christ, making it at times even an effeminate quality. This, coupled with his conception of the superhuman quality of Christ, gave an unnatural interpretation to the suffering of Christ that Bushnell expounded in *Nature and the Supernatural*.[25] He interpreted the anguish of Christ in the garden as "the pathology of a superhuman anguish." [26] Christ overcame this "to go through his most horrible tragedy of the crucifixion, with the serenity of a spectator!" [27] By so doing, he revealed "the depths even of the *passive virtues of God* in his agony and the patience of his suffering love." [28]

These were his ideas concerning Christ's atoning work prior to the completion of his *Christian Nurture* in 1860.

Bushnell made many changes, revisions, and improvements in his theories about Christ after this period.[29] These new insights were embodied in his two-volume work entitled *Vicarious Sacrifice*.[30] In this volume he made clear that it was the resurrection of Christ that served as the clue to the greatness and mystery of Christ's life and death. He referred to the heroic element in Christ and intimated that he had deliberately played this down in order not to obscure the predominance of divinity which he saw in Christ. He realized that an overemphasis on the passivity and submission of Christ could detract from the "grand heroism of his mission."

THE MYSTICAL OR RISEN CHRIST

Since Bushnell was highly mystical and intuitive by nature, he devoted much thought to the mystical or risen Christ. The mystic Christ became a constant part of his life, especially after the vision he had in 1848. In each of his theological treatises a few remarks were made about the effective preaching of Christ and the need for a direct, experiential relationship with Christ.

The titles of his sermons revealed his consuming interest in the mystic Christ. "The Gospel of the Face" proclaimed that "the real Christ is what a Christ may be; what he shall signify in a man's heart." [31] His sermon entitled "The Personal Love and Lead of Christ" showed his conviction that Christ holds a particular relation to individual persons, knows them, loves them, watches over them, leads them individually.[32] The sublime reality of the religious experience was that "Christ has begun to be formed within us," as he explained in his sermon called "Christ, the Form of the Soul." "Live to Christ," he said, "and Christ will live and reign in you." [33] Another volume contained similar themes in his sermons, "Present Relations of Christ with His Followers" and "The Putting on of Christ." [34]

Bushnell's theory of Christian nurture was seriously lacking in the role it gave to Jesus Christ. His Christology would have been more forceful had he lifted up Jesus as a strong and real man with whom young children could identify, and to whom they might give a personal response. Bushnell referred to Jesus several times, but he alternately spoke of the children's need to make responses to the good and right, and to the laws of the home. His failure to appreciate the humanity of Christ, in addition to his recurrent reversion to law, obscured his picture of the total Christ.

If Bushnell had revised his educational theory toward the end of his life, when his theology about Christ had matured, he might have given greater emphasis to the place of Jesus Christ in the Christian education of children and adults. Viewed from the modern perspective, his systematic theology of the doctrine of Christ is inadequate. But in the context of his own day, his provocative insights upon the moral view of the atonement were something of an achievement.

chapter 13 DOCTRINE OF KNOWLEDGE

Most of Bushnell's originality and unorthodox thinking was expressed in his doctrine of knowledge. He had distinctive ideas about communication or the theory of language, and also about the knowledge of truth.

INSIGHTS ABOUT COMMUNICATION

The turning point came with his discovery that "language built on physical images is itself two stories high, and is, in fact, an outfit for a double range of uses." [1] In his "Dissertation" Bushnell undertook an analysis of the origin and usage of language whereby he distinguished between a literal and figurative use of words.[2] He claimed that all language is made up of two departments—the physical and the intellectual.[3] The physical department includes the mere naming of things or actions, and even animals are able to learn these simple representations. But in the second department, symbols or the names of visible things are used as representations of thought and can be learned only "by beings of intelligence (*intus lego*); that is, beings who can read the inner sense, or receive the inner content of words." [4]

This, however, becomes a complicated process. Bushnell pictured the meeting of two primitive, "unlanguaged" men. The mind of the one, laboring with some emotion or thought, would use some figure or symbol of the visible world to be a representation of his thought. Bringing it to the attention of the other, and signifying probably by gesture that he was attempting to communicate his internal state, he would thus prepare the stranger for conceiving or "generating that internal state." "The image becomes, in fact, a common sign or conception of the same internal state—they understand each other," [5] he wrote. Consequently, an "intellectual" word is generated between them, because the symbol now represents not only the physical object but also communicates the thought.

Bushnell was well aware of the complexity of the process and uncovered many of the pitfalls in which men are caught. He knew that the usage and meaning of words depend largely upon the experiences and associations of both the speaker and the hearer. He explained further:

> They have a dictionary meaning that is settled; but yet, hope, fear, love, is to every man what his own life-experience, and his theories, and mental struggles have made it, and he sees it, of necessity, under a color quite peculiar to himself; so peculiar, that he will even advance concerning it, what another cannot find the truth of, or receive.[6]

He pointed up another important truth in the process of communication between persons, by saying:

> Hence, there will be different measures of understanding or misunderstanding, according to the capacity or incapacity, the ingenuousness or moral obliquity of the *receiving party*—even if the communicating party offers only truth, in the best and freshest forms of expression the language provides.[7]

These problems are enhanced, he believed, by the potentiality of words to contain a "latent presence of form" which subtly and unobtrusively creeps in to associate something additional that does not really belong to the thought. This is possible because a word adapted from the physical world and abstracted to convey a mental thought, can have one of these dimensional shades of meaning read back into it when the speaker does not intend such. Because of the mysterious "analogic quality" in life, an association arises between some words —for example, the word right and the word straight, though the former really has no lineal quality to it. Caution is needed, then, to use words as vehicles of thought without letting them impose some latent form which is really extraneous to the thought being communicated.[8]

INTUITIVE KNOWING OF TRUTH

Bushnell also made a crucial discovery about the "knowing" of truths in communicating ideas. Men, according to Bushnell, are always directly confronting God, the universal Author, and do not need to hunt for God by curious arguments and subtle deductions, but abide "in the presence of divine thoughts and meanings." [9] This makes God immediately available and present to man's knowing:

> There is a *perceptive power* in spiritual life, an unction
> of the Holy One, which is itself a kind of inspiration—
> an immediate, experimental knowledge of God, by virtue of which, and partly in the degree of which, Christian theology is possible.[10]

Moreover, man is by nature a mystic being, capable of discerning and reading the hidden meanings of a mystic world, capable of knowing God's spiritual truth.[11] During the controversies over his book *God in Christ*, Bushnell was reported to have told a friend:

> But I conceive of the soul in its living nature; as free,
> and intelligent, and sensitive; as under vital and not mechanical laws. Language, too, for that reason, is not so
> much descriptive as suggestive, being figurative through-

out, even where it deals with spiritual truth. Therefore, *an experience* is needed to interpret words.[12]

IMPLICATIONS FOR THEOLOGY AND NURTURE

Bushnell saw little hope for the development of a meaningful, formal system of dogmatic truth. To attempt that was to make language answer a purpose that was against its nature.[13] He advocated the use of paradoxical statements and contradictory symbols that, in juxtaposition, canceled out the misleading and wrongly imputed "forms" in words and thereby intimated the "whole of truth" behind these symbols. He was intrigued by the way poets such as Coleridge, Goethe, and Bunyan expressed their most inexpressible thoughts "by means of repugnant or somewhat paradoxical epithets." [14] He concluded, "Poets, then, are the true metaphysicians, and if there be any complete science of man to come, they must bring it." [15] It is singular that Bushnell arrived at this need for paradox in the expression of spiritual truth at approximately the same time as Sören Kierkegaard (1813–55).

Creeds and catechisms did not greatly impress Bushnell. Too often they had become formulas and rigid statements to be taken literally. Most theological disputes originated because the differing parties failed to separate truths from their forms, or to see that the same essential truth could be clothed under forms that are contradictory.

In rejecting the creeds as "guards and tests of purity," he apparently failed to realize that the early church had sought to preserve the essentials of its faith in paradoxical statements similar to those he was proposing. He chafed at the creedal statements about the Trinity and the person of Christ, as though he had missed their significance. If he had been more familiar with church history and had been more successful at bringing his many insights into a consistent whole, if he had been able to modify some of his enthusiasms, he might not have fallen into some of his most grievous errors. His failure to achieve coherence at various points detracted considerably from the impact of his valuable insights.

Bushnell hoped that in the future his new theories of language and knowledge would achieve two results: "a more comprehensive, friendly, and fraternal state" among different groups of Christians; and a new conviction, among Christian believers everywhere, that truth in its highest and freest forms is intuitive—spirit and life, as Christ had declared—and not bound by dogmas and formulas.[16]

Although he was outspoken against mathematical types of formulas and dogmas in religion, he did acknowledge the need for theology—if constructed with care and wisdom. Though he emphasized the intuitive aspect of religion, his realistic nature caused him to say:

> Considering that Christian character is imperfect, liable to the instigation of passion, to be overheated in the flesh and think it the inspiration of God, Christian theology and speculative activity are needed as providing checks and balances for the life, to save it from visionary flights, erratic fancies, and wild hallucinations.[17]

He viewed theology as a preparation for faith, as a necessary unifying of opinions and beliefs, as an apologetic for the Christian religion, as a mode of relating the facts of Christianity to the other intellectual disciplines of life.[18]

Bushnell's view of the intuitive side of knowledge added a new depth to his educational theory. The drill in catechism and the memorization of scripture verses had long been the central method of religious education in New England. His critics were distressed by Bushnell's apparent disregard for the doctrinal teaching of children. The theory held by parents was that if the child's head were filled with opinions and dogmas, these would then regulate life. Bushnell contended that the opposite is true; that the heart controls the issues of life. He knew that doctrinal training could have some preparatory effect upon a child's mind, but the quality of religion exemplified in the home has the greatest influence on the development of faith. His epistemological insight into the distinction between the knowledge "of" God and the knowledge "about" God, between a direct, intuitive knowledge of God and a reflected knowledge of theology, had an important effect upon his theory of nurture.

Bushnell also proposed that a child needed experiences within his family during his prelanguage years, from which he could intuit meanings. When the child *then* reached the age of words, and finally of concepts, these meanings could be symbolized and expressed. From this base it was possible to develop the intuited meanings of personal relationships into a fuller knowledge of God, and into a more mature faith. In his educational theory Bushnell maintained that "no truth is really taught by words, or interpreted by intellectual and logical methods; truth must be lived into meaning, before it can be truly known." [19]

chapter 14 DOCTRINE OF RELIGIOUS EXPERIENCE

Horace Bushnell had a clear understanding of the nature of religious experience within the Christian life. If his early writings about Christian nurture had not made his position clear on this point, the sermons and books that followed during the remainder of his life left no doubt about the matter. Although he accentuated regeneration, his views were radically different from those of his contemporaries, whether they were revivalistic Calvinists or Unitarians.

A religious experience meant a radical turning back to God, a deep and thorough transformation of the life and spirit. He declared in 1848 that the aim of Christianity was to "bring us off from the self-centers about which we revolve in our sins, and set us moving as in God." [1] But God could not inspire a soul or have personal relationships with it while it was "hugging itself" and "habitually set on having its own ways." [2] Bushnell stated:

> A *great revolution* is so far needed, therefore, if it is to find God; for God cannot be revealed in it, or born in it, save when it comes away from all its lower ends to be in God's. No movings of mere natural sentiment reach this point. Nothing but a *voluntary surrender* of the whole life to his will prepares it to be set in this open relation to God. [3]

MAN'S CAPACITY FOR RESPONSE

Within this new framework for religious experience, there was a great need for the exercise of human faith. For Bushnell, God does not strike through to human souls by force of "fiat-power," but by his moral power working through attractions and impressions which can be either resisted or accepted.[4] The inducements of God as manifested by the human life and death of Christ won the consent and trust of the new believer. This trust or faith opens the way for God's transforming power "to bring the soul up into victory over itself and seal it as the heir of God." [5] The person is thus "reconnected" with the divine nature, "atoned, reconciled with God, transformed by the inward touch of God's feeling and character." [6] This is the "power of God unto salvation," this is "justification by faith."

Bushnell put great emphasis on the power and need of man to practice this faith. Such practice involves the negative aspect of vigorous self-renunciation, of creating a void within the life which God might fill. It involves a positive "reaching after God, an offering up of the soul to him that he may come and dwell in it and consecrate it as his temple." [7] Mostly, however, Bushnell stressed the personal quality of faith. There was a place for beliefs and notional truths and doctrines *about* Christ and God, but the real core of faith did not concern these. "It is the act of trust by which one being, a sinner, commits himself to another being, a Savior," he wrote.[8] Elsewhere, he strongly reaffirmed this same personal quality of faith:

> No, the faith that brings salvation is the act of a being toward a being, sinner to Savior, man to God. . . . It is the act of an undone, lost man, giving himself over in trust to Jesus Christ, person to person; a total consenting to Christ, to be of him, and with him, and for him, to let him heal and renovate, and govern. . . . The simple first point of it is Christ, a Savior, manifested in such love and divinity that, taken for salvation as a being, he can be trusted. And when he is thus trusted, that is faith. . . . Saving faith is person trusted to person—that and nothing else.[9]

IMMEDIATE KNOWLEDGE OF GOD

In the thought of Bushnell, a return to God leads to an immediate knowledge of God. Just as a man has a direct and intuitive knowledge of himself—a "self-feeling,"—so he comes to an intuitive "felt consciousness of God," to an immediate sense of God's presence.[10] Thus, faith opens the sensitivity and receptivity of a man to receive what should have been the "original and always normal revelation," if sin had not intervened. Man has been created to live in this immediate consciousness of God,[11] for God is the very "complement" of his being and without God he only half exists.[12]

A NEW DISPOSITION

Religious experience, in Bushnell's theology, leads to a new state in man. It leads to a new disposition, a new ruling love, a new "derivative" state of righteousness. Regeneration, therefore, is not the insertion of a new man into the old, nor the total recreation of the old. It has to be a change and regeneration of the same man in a way that preserves personal identity. The strong analogies of the Scriptures about "putting off the old man and putting on the new man" are not to be taken too literally.[13]

He attempted to explain it by likening it to the change of the "governing purpose" in a man, which would effect a change in his whole life and character. Yet, he realized that this analogy was not really adequate, for a man by his own will could change his governing purpose without any supernatural remedy or power from beyond.[14] Bushnell defined regeneration as the restoration of a "living connection with God" (that has been lost through sin) which changes the "wrong love" to a "right love" and thereby works the radical transformation of the original man.[15]

MATURING THE NEW CHARACTER

Keenly aware of the joy and ecstasy of the newly found relationship with God through Christ, Bushnell was yet realistic and sensible. All is not attained in this first momentous event of restoration. The new believer is, he felt, the same person as

111

before, having the same conscience and remembering the same sins. It is true that his new consciousness of God makes him feel like a new creature,[16] but this new consciousness has to be ratified and stabilized in the fabric of his character and within activities of everyday life.

In his sermon entitled "Regeneration," he spoke of this "process of growth and gradual advancement":

> For it is only potentially that the new life is regarded as a complete or total renovation. As the child is potentially a man, as the seed is potentially the full-grown plant, so it is with the regenerated life in Christ. . . . All such conceptions of growth fall into place *under* the fact that the new character begun is only begun, and that while it is the root and spring of a complete renovation, it must needs unfold itself and fill itself out into completeness, by a process of holy living.[17]

In another sermon, "The True Problem of Christian Experience," [18] he indicated that the new Christian is changed in the very "citizenship" of his soul. Yet he knew how easily temptations return; how "fluctuating moods, bad thoughts, unmanageable doubts" press in upon the soul like "a whole army of secret invaders"; how panic can easily grip the soul in its unfamiliar situation.[19] He believed that through the struggles of everyday life the "new love" has to be developed into a "fixed state." [20] Here, again, he repeated an idea that he had expressed in his earliest writings about Christian nurture: "No state of virtue is complete, however total the virtue, save as it is won by a conflict with evil, and fortified by the struggles of a resolute and even bitter experience." [21] The Christian life thus requires a continuous response to God, a continuous appropriation of God's power and righteousness.

He was aware also of the sinfulness and imperfection of the church; he knew that included within church membership are many disagreeable people. But he thought a Christian should not be disillusioned when he discovered that the church is not perfect. "Our relations of church brotherhood," he said, "are a continual drill in and for society." [22] The training received within the church fellowship is to prove a leavening influence upon society as a whole, and also a preparation for God's "Eternal Society." Bushnell compared the divine society being formed within the church to "God's hospital." In it God is watching and nursing "his poor morally broken children," loving them not for what they are, but only for what he can make of them.[23]

According to Bushnell, the worship experience of the Christian should be a direct communication of the soul with God, an intuitive knowledge and immediate awareness of his presence. Preaching ought to exhibit the facts of Christ's life and set forth the meaning of his character in such a way as to bring worshipers directly into the presence of God.[24]

In God alone is man's strength and salvation. Man is totally dependent upon God. In such ideas as these, Bushnell's thought was very close to the New Testament faith and the beliefs of the historical church. He did not advocate a salvation by human education alone. For Bushnell, the source of grace needed by man was strictly supernatural. His theory of nurture was based upon regeneration, upon a significant doctrine of religious experience.

PART IV   PERSPECTIVES
AND EVALUATIONS

---

chapter 15 RETROSPECT:
THE INFLUENCE
OF BUSHNELL'S
THOUGHT
ON AMERICAN
THEOLOGIANS

In order to understand Bushnell's significance in Christian education, some attention must be given to his place in the development of American theology.   Because he was a provocative
thinker who touched on a wide range of theological issues, several major studies would be needed to trace thoroughly the
manner in which subsequent thinkers adopted some of his ideas
or ignored his useful distinctions.

EVALUATIONS BY FRIENDS AND ADMIRERS
Bushnell's works were read extensively in his day, due in part
to the lively controversies that appeared in many of the religious
periodicals of New England, and to the freshness of his approach to many religious questions.   His doctrine of Christian
nurture, and the charges of heresy concerning his volume *God
in Christ*, stirred up a clamor among the reading public.[1]
Reuen Thomas, speaking of Bushnell's influence in England,
said that "all young ministers of any alertness of mind, in all
denominations, read his books." [2]

In 1880, a few years after Bushnell's death, *The New Englander* carried a review of his biography written by his daughter.[3] The length of this review—sixty-three pages—indicates the esteem in which he was held.

Amos S. Chesebrough, who had been a close friend of Bushnell, wrote in 1886 a thoughtful article in *The Andover Review* entitled, "The Theological Opinions of Horace Bushnell as Related to His Character and Christian Experience." [4] This was a careful evaluation of the fundamental tenets around which Bushnell's views revolved.

A. J. William Myers has gathered together many statements and favorable comments concerning Bushnell from a wide range of sources.[5] Along with these references he reports that Phillips Brooks had absorbed much of his theology and that Bushnell's *Sermons for the New Life* showed the signs of being one of the most used books in Brooks' library.[6]

Washington Gladden was also deeply influenced by Bushnell.[7] He states in his *Recollections*: "Dr. Bushnell was, beyond a question, the greatest theological genius of the American church in the nineteenth century.[8]

Edwin D. Mead, editor of *The New England Magazine*, wrote in the December, 1899, issue that Bushnell had been "a great light and a positive guide" to many thoughtful and influential preachers in the "religious turmoil and confusion" of the previous generation.

Theodore Munger was another whom Bushnell greatly influenced. Indeed, he wrote the second major treatment of Bushnell's life. In his book of 1899, which was not given to overstatement, he stated:

> We cannot pass by *Christian Nurture* as it appears in the later full edition without once more calling attention to it as an achievement in the world of New England theology. In point of influence, it is second only to that of Edwards in which he ended the union of church and state by reassertion of man's individual relations to God. . . . The greatness of the book as an

intellectual achievement has not had full recognition, chiefly because its theological surroundings have not been understood. . . . For it cannot be denied that the conception of spiritual regeneration, and of its means and methods, which prevailed at the time has largely passed away, and that everything except the simple need of it has yielded to a conception based upon and composed chiefly of religious nurture. The various theories of depravity, of the will, of divine grace, of the action of the Holy Spirit, of sanctification, have either disappeared, or been so altered as hardly to be recognized.[9]

In 1902 the famous church historian Williston Walker spoke at the celebration of the Bushnell Centenary in the General Association of Connecticut, concluding with these words:

> Dr. Bushnell was not a theologian in the sense in which that other great son of Connecticut, Jonathan Edwards, was a theologian. He had no desire to be. He wrought out no close-argued logical system. He believed none possible. . . . He founded no school in the technical sense. No party among us calls itself by his name. But he had a poet's fire of imagination, and a prophet's perception of the reality of God. . . . He moved by the strong impulse of original and constructive genius along lines which *Christian thought in other lands* has to a considerable extent been traversing. . . . He sought to make the presentation of Christianity simpler and more natural. And for all these reasons *he has been increasingly a power in religious thinking among us.* His work has touched and strengthened and broadened many a mind that has been unable to accept his presentations of truth in their fullness. His has been a great influence. *He has made easy* for many the transition from the older to the newer conceptions of the Christian faith.[10]

Writing in 1919, John Wright Buckham classed Bushnell as one of the "liberators" of religious thought in America and marked him "as one of those creative minds whose mission is to enkindle others." [11] Buckham comments:

Bushnell was in some respects almost as truly the father of the later constructive development of American theology as was Jonathan Edwards of the earlier. . . . The last twenty-five years have witnessed a greatly enhanced estimate of his part in theological advance and a fresh sense of the unexhausted treasures of his productive personality.[12]

Frank Hugh Foster's work *The Modern Movement in American Theology,* written in 1934 and published posthumously in 1939, dealt also with Bushnell's influence. Foster writes:

He was a seer rather than a systematic and logical thinker. . . . Radical as he seemed to be, he was *for the most part a great conservative,* accepting the Bible and a large portion of the Christian system as it was handed on to him without special question.[13]

CRITICAL ASSESSMENTS

The comments about Bushnell became more severe with the rise of neo-orthodoxy and the dissatisfaction concerning American liberalism. In 1934 Walter Marshall Horton made this comment in his book *Realistic Theology:*

With Parker and Bushnell, in fact, there came into American theology that selfsame distrust of abstract reason, that selfsame trust in moral faith and religious intuition which had worked such a revolution in German theology a half century earlier. . . . The philosophy which the great Unitarian and the great Congregationalist derived from these sources was substantially the same: an *idealistic monism* which broke down the old barriers between reason and revelation, natural and supernatural, secular and sacred, and found God immanent in all things.[14]

Horton summarized his opinions by saying that "the theology of Bushnell is essentially identical with that liberal theology which is passing away before our eyes." [15]

In 1940 George Hammar echoed the sentiments of Walter Marshall Horton. He mentioned that Bushnell's theology was similar to that of Albrecht Ritschl and, indeed, that American theologians sometimes quoted Ritschl when they were really indebted to the influence of Bushnell. He reiterated Horton's views concerning what had been termed Bushnell's "idealistic monism" and his "immanent conception of God." He concluded that if American liberal theology could be defined as an "idealistic monism" which broke down the barrier between reason and revelation, then Bushnell could be classed as the "pioneer" of such a theology.[16]

RENEWED APPRECIATION

More recent evaluations of Bushnell's thought have brought forth a careful discernment and a new tenor. In 1937 H. Richard Niebuhr was dealing with the naïve optimism of the liberalism which held that "a God without wrath brought man without sin into a kingdom without judgment through the ministrations of a Christ without a cross." [17] But then he proceeded to add a qualifying note to his consideration of liberalism:

> The temper of evolutionary optimism did not prevail in all parts of the liberal movement. There were mediators who shared the protest against static versions of divine sovereignty, salvation, and Christian hope but sought nevertheless to retain the critical and dialectical elements in Protestantism. Of these Horace Bushnell was the greatest.[18]

Niebuhr went on to say that Bushnell's theory of nurture represented a protest against the mechanization of conversion and also a recognition of the principle of growth. He was also quick to say that Bushnell still recognized the necessity of regeneration and believed that the way in which Bushnell rejected Unitarianism, and the manner in which he wrestled for years with the problem of the atonement, were evidences of the fact

118

that the "discontinuities in life" were very real to Bushnell. He was convinced that Bushnell fully recognized the need for the "revolutionary" elements of Christianity. And so Niebuhr concluded: "Though the prevailing tone of his theology was romantic and liberal, the Protestant and evangelical note was not lost." [19]

This new note in the appraisal of Bushnell's place within American theology has been substantiated and worked out more explicitly in the Yale study of E. Clinton Gardner entitled "Man as Sinner in Nineteenth Century New England: A Study in the Challenge of Romantic Humanitarianism." [20] In this study Gardner maintains that whereas the traditional Calvinists had been defensive thinkers, and the Unitarian liberals had been negative in their evaluation of orthodox Protestantism, Bushnell represented a third element which made a more constructive approach to the theological issues that arose during the transitional period in New England theology.

Gardner complains that the positive insights which Bushnell proclaimed from his independent position were largely overlooked by his successors who were inclined to interpret him in terms of William Ellery Channing. He points out that the "romantic humanitarianism," which had developed in reaction to the encrustations of Calvinism and the rationalism of the earlier deism, had become a real threat to orthodox Christianity. It was a special threat to the Christian doctrine of man because its optimism suggested that man by his efforts was able to perfect his nature without the aid of transcendent grace.

Gardner shows that Bushnell achieved a significant "reconstruction" of the doctrine of sin which neither the Calvinists nor the Unitarians were able to achieve. He points out that Bushnell's great contribution was his new doctrine of man in which he displaced the concept of natural ability and moral inability for the "concept of response." His exposition shows forth the wholesome nature of Bushnell's doctrine of man, of sin, and of regeneration. He points out what several other writers failed to see; namely, that while Bushnell's close followers were greatly helped and influenced by him, they misinterpreted him on numerous points and departed from many of his important insights.

It is not surprising in the light of these critical estimates that there is today a renewed interest in the thought and continuing influence of Horace Bushnell. Within this larger framework, an understanding of Bushnell's place in American theology is a necessary prelude for evaluating his significance within the field of Christian education. The value and balance of his theological insights have been largely overlooked, and only now in the second half of the twentieth century are his accomplishments being more fully appreciated.

chapter 16 RETROSPECT:
BUSHNELL'S
INFLUENCE UPON
CHRISTIAN
EDUCATION
IN AMERICA

Some assessment needs to be made of Bushnell's influence within the various historical developments that occurred in the Christian educational movement in America.

A. J. William Myers offers a preliminary note of caution which serves as a springboard to such an investigation:

> At the outset it should be made clear that Bushnell was not familiar with educational techniques. He was a prophet and preacher who saw certain fundamental ideas clearly without always realizing their full implication.[1]

As indicated previously, a new attitude toward children had begun to develop even prior to Bushnell's writing. His theory of nurture gave new impetus to the change and stirred up immediate theological controversy, yet "its practical suggestions in regard to Christian nurture have waited more than three quarters of a century to be fully recognized in the theory and practice of religious education."[2]

INFLUENCE ON WRITERS

Bushnell was a personal friend of Henry Clay Trumbull, who played a very important role in the development of the Sunday school movement in America during its early years. In telling of Bushnell's influence, which served to bring him "out from the bondage of dead literalism," Trumbull writes:

> His greatest service to me, as it has been to many another, was in bringing me to see that God's message or gift to us in the Scriptures is a gift to our "imagination," rather than to our positive knowledge; that Bible truth, at the best, suggests to us far more than it can define.[3]

Bushnell tried repeatedly to get Trumbull out of Sunday school work and into what he felt was the more important task of the pastorate. Bushnell's experience with the Massachusetts Sabbath School had not been a happy one and the objectives of the Sunday school movement were contrary to his theory of nurture. Toward the end of his life, Bushnell came to have a higher respect for the Sunday school movement and Trumbull prevailed upon him to preach the opening sermon at the 1869 convention of the Connecticut Sunday school workers. Bushnell's sermon was entitled "God's Thoughts, Fit Bread for Children," and it was later published. Other than this, Bushnell had very little contact with the Sunday school movement.

Though Trumbull gives evidence of comprehending Bushnell's ideas about the regeneration of children and the personal relationship to a "Being" as the essence of the Christian life,[4] Bushnell's nurture theory did not seem to displace the revivalistic aim and method employed by the Sunday school. Harrison S. Elliott states:

> During the entire period from the inauguration of the Sunday school movement in the first quarter of the nineteenth century down to the close of the century, the controlling purpose was to make the doctrinal message of the Bible known to children and youth. . . . Conversion at the age of accountability was the purpose of

the Sunday school, and little or no attention was given
to nurture of Christian life and conduct either before
or after conversion.[5]

Francis E. Clark, who originated and sponsored the Young
People's Society of Christian Endeavor which began in 1881,
acknowledged his indebtedness to Bushnell's theory. In his
book *The Children and the Church*, he vigorously proclaimed:

> It is natural, it is possible, it is desirable for children to
> grow up into Christian manhood and womanhood with-
> out experiencing any sharp and sudden transition from
> an evil life to a good life. Nay, it is not only possible
> and desirable, it is the thing we ought to expect; it
> ought to be as common for young children to be born
> into the kingdom of God as to be born into the world.
> It is possible and natural for children to be converted
> at their mother's knee, and never know the time when
> they did not love the Savior.[6]

Amos S. Chesebrough was also much impressed with Bushnell's nurture theory. He had entered into the defense of
Bushnell during the controversy over the latter's *Discourses on
Christian Nurture* and a close personal friendship developed.[7]
In 1883 Chesebrough published a book entitled *Children
Trained for Discipleship*.[8] It incorporated several of Bushnell's
ideas, though its emphasis on conversion and its catechetical
suggestions for children concerning "awakening," "conviction,"
"salvation," and "repentance," would not pass present-day curriculum standards for children.[9]

THE EDUCATIONAL FERMENT IN AMERICA

The arrival of the educational ideas of Pestalozzi, Froebel, and
Herbart into America produced a new ferment in all phases of
education. Together with the new biblical criticism, these ideas
spotlighted deficiencies in curriculum materials (such as the
Uniform Lesson Series adopted in 1872) and stimulated a whole
series of curriculum revisions within the churches. The psychological findings of men such as G. Stanley Hall, William

James, and Edward L. Thorndike soon burst upon the scene. Then along came the research of Hugh Hartshorne and Mark May, plus that of William H. Kilpatrick. Famous educators such as John Dewey, George Albert Coe, William C. Bower, and George Herbert Betts also influenced the thought patterns of the day through their creative work.

In the many curriculum changes that took place there occurred a complete changeover from the old "Bible-centered" approach to a new "experience-centered" approach. The new experiential type of religious education was very much an incorporation of the ideas of progressive education. Adelaide Teague Case points out that Bushnell opened the way for a planned program of religious guidance, but that the early selection of materials for different age levels was based upon the "culture epoch theory" of G. Stanley Hall.[10] The engrossment of the educators with new psychological and educational ideas in the late eighteenth and early nineteenth centuries served to crowd out the theological premises of a system of nurture in the Christian life. Bushnell had perceived many psychological truths but in his theory of nurture he had thoroughly embedded them in the basic truths of the historic church.

In 1903, in Chicago, the first meeting of the Religious Education Association was held. This meeting drew together representatives from many church denominations and experts from the field of general education, whose sole purpose was to promote the best type of religious education. The speeches given on this occasion are an excellent indication of the thinking of that period. Several references were made to Bushnell and some statements reflected the influence of his nurture theory.

George Albert Coe, especially, made statements that were reminiscent of Bushnell's words:

> The central fact of the modern educational movement is recognition of the child as a determining factor in the whole educational scheme. The child is a living organism, *a being that grows from within by assimilation, not from without by accretion.*[11]

But Coe, like many other speakers at this convention, had accepted the "recapitulation" theory of G. Stanley Hall because he stated: "The individual is said to recapitulate the history of his race. It follows that the mighty power and pervasiveness of religion in general are to be looked for in miniature in child life." [12] But another statement incorporated directly the words of Bushnell: "We must never regard either home or church as normally successful until it is no longer the exception but the rule for children to 'grow up Christians, and never to know themselves as being otherwise.'" [13]

Whereas Coe concluded his famous statement with the words of Bushnell, drawing upon the immanence of God which Bushnell had also expounded, he neglected the transcendence and personal nature of God which Bushnell had taught. Although Coe advocated a growth from within instead of accretion, he changed Bushnell's concept of growth when he placed it upon the recapitulation theory.

There is no evidence in Coe's statement of the terrific struggle between good and evil, obedience and sin, nor of the response to a personal God which was part of Bushnell's concept of personal growth. There is no mention in Coe of the fall of man and the bondage of sin, which requires a supernatural remedy, a regenerative process. His idea of growth, recapitulation, and the man "performed" in the child, sound suspiciously like the educement or "drawing out" of the good and natural powers within a child which Bushnell had disavowed.[14]

In 1929 George Albert Coe spoke of religious education as the reconstruction of relations between persons guided by the "hypothesis" of the existence of God, the "Great Valuer of Persons." [15] In 1925 William C. Bower had spoken of religious education as the creative effort of building a social order in fellowship with God as "the Creator of Values." [16] This certainly was not the conception of God upon which Bushnell based his theory of nurture. The theology of these two key educators within the church was radically different from that of Bushnell. Yet writers such as A. J. William Myers and Harrison S. Elliott have appropriated Bushnell and placed him squarely in the camp of the extremely liberal theologians and the progressive educators.[17]

In direct contrast to the interpretation made of Bushnell's theory of Christian nurture by liberal educators is the usage made of his ideas by Edward Payson Hammond in his book entitled *The Conversion of Children*.[18] He quotes Bushnell to gain authority for the nurturing of children in the Christian faith at an early age, and points out that the Moravians raised their children so that they could not remember any time when they began to be religious. As a children's evangelist, Hammond is particularly pleased to find that Bushnell believed children were sinners in need of the forgiveness and grace of Christ. Although he quotes Bushnell approvingly, his accounts of the conversion experiences of children are of the type that Bushnell had strongly opposed! All too frequently writers have seized upon the label of Bushnell's theory or have extracted certain phrases and ideas from his theory without having grasped the overall significance of his understanding of Christian nurture.

A MODERATE INFLUENCE

A certain amount of Bushnell's influence, however, has carried over into the Christian education movement in America, but not in the extreme liberal or conservative wings. This moderate sphere of influence is more difficult to establish but may be best represented by the work and writing of a man such as Luther A. Weigle.

In 1911, in words that have a real affinity to Bushnell's thoughts, Luther A. Weigle wrote:

> The final goal of our work is spiritual. No mere accretion of knowledge or outward molding of action can save the world or bring a single soul to fullness of life. . . . The true teacher is an evangelist. He is not content merely to teach *about* God. . . . He seeks to help his pupils to *know* God in personal relation and so to love and serve him.[19]

126

In 1924 Weigle wrote an excellent and inclusive summary of Bushnell's Christian nurture in the February issue of *Religious Education*. Weigle served as the Horace Bushnell Professor of Christian Nurture at Yale from 1916 to 1924, and then as the Sterling Professor of Religious Education at Yale from 1924 to 1929.

In an address prepared for delivery in 1929 to the International Missionary Council at Jerusalem,[20] and again in a book published in 1939 entitled *Jesus and the Educational Method*,[21] he said that the need of the world was not evangelism or religious education, but rather evangelism through Christian education. He mentioned that he would not surrender the term religious education to a few who thought of it as "educing of natural good" in humans and who failed to acknowledge ultimate dependence upon the Spirit of God. Nor would he surrender the term evangelism to itinerant revivalists or to preachers. He felt that the evangel was the content of the Christian message and the character of Christian motive—it did not refer to a method.

In 1940 there was issued under his chairmanship a statement of basic philosophy by a subcommittee of the International Council of Religious Education. The first three objectives in the statement have similarities to earlier statements of Weigle, and are quite different from the statements of the educational philosophy of the previous two decades:

1. Christian education seeks to foster in growing persons a consciousness of God as a reality in human experience, and a sense of personal relationship with him.

2. Christian education seeks to develop in growing persons such an understanding and appreciation of the personality, life, and teaching of Jesus as will lead to experience of him as Savior and Lord, loyalty to him and his cause, and will manifest itself in daily life and conduct.

3. Christian education seeks to foster in growing persons a progressive and continuous development of Christlike character.[22]

Finally, in 1947, Weigle wrote a lengthy and commendatory introduction to a new edition of Bushnell's *Christian Nurture*,[23] in order to give it fresh prominence.

In 1947 another subcommittee of the International Council of Christian Education published its findings concerning the need for more theological concepts in Christian education. In a manner far removed from that of the optimistic liberalism of former years, the council began to discuss the relationship of certain theological doctrines to the educational task.[24] Commenting upon this work and other developments, James D. Smart announced in 1954: "We stand, then, at the beginning of a new period of development, the period of theological recovery." [25]

Among the recent books endeavoring to formulate an educational approach rooted in sound theology, few have paid much attention to Bushnell's *Christian Nurture*. Several writers have made brief and commendatory remarks about it, some have repeated his famous phrases, but none have given evidence of thoroughly comprehending his work or of incorporating any of his insights into their own writing.

For the most part, Horace Bushnell has been either bypassed or misinterpreted. His immediate successors failed to understand his theory of nurture or else were unable to implement his insights. Christian education became dominated by the new psychology and the new pedagogic methods. Bushnell's title of "nurture" was often used, plus his idea that the Christian life did not need to begin with a "spiritual convulsion," but his successors appropriated only those elements of his thought which they preferred, ignoring the wholesome balance of his underlying theology. Certain educators have appropriated him as their kin, but in the process they have actually twisted his doctrines of growth and the immanence of God to their own liking. Horace Bushnell still waits to be rediscovered in the depth of his thought and appropriated properly for the vast enrichment of contemporary Christian education.

NOTES

introduction

1. Randolph Crump Miller, *Education for Christian Living* (Englewood Cliffs, N.J.: Prentice-Hall, 1956), p. 31; Harrison S. Elliott, *Can Religious Education Be Christian?* (New York: Macmillan, 1940), p. 33.

2. For samples of such tributes see George Stewart, *A History of Religious Education in Connecticut to the Middle of the Nineteenth Century*, eds. Luther A. Weigle and Henry B. Wright, "Yale Studies in the History and Theory of Religious Education" (New Haven: Yale University Press, 1924), I, 347, 356 f.; Sandford Fleming, *Children and Puritanism: The Place of Children in the Life and Thought of the New England Churches, 1620–1847*, "Yale Studies in Religious Education" (New Haven: Yale University Press, 1933), VIII, 207 f.; A. J. William Myers, *Horace Bushnell and Religious Education* (Boston: Manthorne and Burack, Inc., 1937), pp. 1 f., also chap. 7, "The Judgment of History," pp. 148–77.

3. Elliott, *op. cit.*, p. 32.

4. Miller, *op. cit.*, p. 30.

5. Horace Bushnell, *Christian Nurture* (New York: Charles Scribner's Sons, 1862).

6. Horace Bushnell, *Views of Christian Nurture and of Subjects Adjacent Thereto* (Hartford, Conn.: Edwin Hunt, 1847), pp. 98 f.

chapter 1

1. Mary Bushnell Cheney, *Life and Letters of Horace Bushnell* (New York: Harper & Bros., 1880); Barbara M. Cross, *Horace Bushnell: Minister to a Changing America* (Chicago: University of

Chicago Press, 1958); Rachel Henderlite, "The Theological Basis of Horace Bushnell's Christian Nurture" (unpublished Ph.D. dissertation, Yale University, 1947), pp. 1–56; Theodore T. Munger, *Horace Bushnell: Preacher and Theologian* (Boston: Houghton Mifflin, 1899).

2. Cheney, *op. cit.*, pp. 40 f.

3. *Ibid.*, p. 456.

4. Horace Bushnell, *God in Christ: Three Discourses Delivered at New Haven, Cambridge, and Andover, with a Preliminary Dissertation on Language* (centenary ed.; New York: Charles Scribner's Sons, 1910), p. 73.

5. Cheney, *op. cit.*, p. 295.

6. *Ibid.*, pp. 19 f.

7. Horace Bushnell, *The Vicarious Sacrifice, Grounded in Principles Interpreted by Human Analogies*, Vol. II (New York: Charles Scribner's Sons, 1891).

8. Cheney, *op. cit.*, pp. 15 f.

9. *Ibid.*, p. 105.

10. *Ibid.*, pp. 192 f.

11. Horace Bushnell, *The Spirit in Man: Sermons and Selections* (centenary ed.; New York: Charles Scribner's Sons, 1903), pp. 39–51.

12. Horace Bushnell, *Sermons for the New Life* (2d ed.; New York: Charles Scribner's Sons, 1858), pp. 95, 102.

13. Horace Bushnell, *Sermons on Living Subjects* (New York: Charles Scribner's Sons, 1887), p. 182.

14. Horace Bushnell, *Nature and the Supernatural, as Together Constituting the One System of God* (New York: Charles Scribner's Sons, 1860).

15. Horace Bushnell, *Views of Christian Nurture and of Subjects Adjacent Thereto* (Hartford, Conn.: Edwin Hunt, 1847), pp. 5–47. These discourses were originally published by the Massachusetts Sabbath School Society, but following a charge of heresy against them they were quickly suspended. Bushnell promptly republished the discourses on his own initiative in an expanded volume.

16. Horace Bushnell, *Christian Nurture* (New York: Charles Scribner's Sons, 1862).

17. Horace Bushnell, "Spiritual Economy of Revivals of Religion," *The Quarterly Christian Spectator*, X (1838), 131–48.

18. The second work was designed to correct the first volume. But the parts of the first volume that had been revised were never deleted. The demand of friends brought about the combination of the two volumes in their entirety under a revised title. Bushnell, *The Vicarious Sacrifice, Grounded in Principles Interpreted by Human Analogies* (2 vols.), *op. cit.*

chapter 2

1. In the author's notes, comparisons will be made to modern books that relate to some of the ideas which Bushnell propounded. While many of Bushnell's ideas were germinal and preliminary, there is a relationship between them and the detailed knowledge of recent books.

2. See Isle Forest, *Child Development* (New York: Mc-Graw-Hill, 1954); Arnold Gesell, Frances L. Ilg, et al., *Child Development: An Introduction to the Study of Human Growth*; Vol. I, *Infant and Child in the Culture of Today*; Vol. II, *The Child from Five to Ten* (2 vols. in 1 ed.; New York: Harper & Bros., 1949); Robert J. Havighurst, *Developmental Tasks and Education* (New York: Longmans, Green and Co., 1952); Elizabeth B. Hurlock, *Child Development* (2d ed.; New York: McGraw-Hill, 1950); Sidney L. Pressey and Raymond G. Kuhlen, *Psychological Development Through the Life Span* (New York: Harper & Bros., 1957).

3. Horace Bushnell, *Christian Nurture* (New York: Charles Scribner's Sons, 1862), pp. 233 f.

4. Cf. Forest, *op. cit.*, chap. 15, "Ego Development," pp. 242–50; Erik H. Erikson, *Childhood and Society* (New York: W. W. Norton & Co., 1950), pp. 207 f., 237–431; Harry Stack Sullivan, *The Interpersonal Theory of Psychiatry*, eds. Helen Swick Perry and Mary Ladd Gawel (New York: W. W. Norton & Co., 1953), pp. 158–71.

5. Bushnell, *op. cit.*, p. 28. Italics added.

6. *Ibid.*

7. *Ibid.*, p. 324. Italics added. Cf. Margaret A. Ribble,

chap. 1, "The Right to a Mother," *The Rights of Infants: Early Psychological Needs and Their Satisfaction* (New York: Columbia University Press, 1943).

8. *Ibid.,* p. 250.

9. *Ibid.,* p. 240. Italics added. Cf. Gesell, Ilg, et al., *op. cit.,* I, 31 f.

10. Bushnell, *op. cit.,* p. 240. Cf. Basil A. Yeaxlee, *Religion and the Growing Mind* (London: Nisbet and Co., 1939), p. 57.

11. Bushnell, *op. cit.,* pp. 257 f. Cf. Dorothy W. Baruch, *One Little Boy* (New York: Julian Press, 1952).

12. Bushnell, *op. cit.,* p. 298. Cf. Yeaxlee, *op. cit.,* pp. 55 f.; Lewis Joseph Sherrill, *The Struggle of the Soul* (New York: Macmillan, 1950), pp. 40 ff.

13. Bushnell, *op. cit.,* pp. 247 f.

14. *Ibid.,* p. 246. Cf. Dorothy W. Baruch, *New Ways in Discipline: You and Your Child Today* (New York: McGraw-Hill, 1949), pp. 46 ff., 71 ff.

15. Bushnell, *op. cit.,* p. 245. Italics added.

16. *Ibid.,* p. 317.

17. *Ibid.,* pp. 248 f.

chapter 3

1. Horace Bushnell, *Christian Nurture* (New York: Charles Scribner's Sons, 1862), p. 145.

2. *Ibid.,* pp. 233 f.

3. *Ibid.,* p. 11.

4. *Ibid.,* p. 321. Cf. Basil A. Yeaxlee, *Religion and the Growing Mind* (London: Nisbet and Co., 1939), pp. 88–118.

5. Bushnell, *op. cit.,* p. 383. Cf. Yeaxlee, *op. cit.,* pp. 81, 85.

6. Bushnell, *op. cit.,* p. 339. Cf. Elizabeth B. Hurlock, *Child Development* (2d ed.; New York: McGraw-Hill, 1950), pp. 337–89.

7. Bushnell, *op. cit.,* pp. 340 f.

8. *Ibid.,* p. 347.

9. *Ibid.*, p. 315.

10. *Ibid.*

11. *Ibid.*, p. 317.

12. *Ibid.*, p. 326.

13. *Ibid.*, pp. 296 f.

14. *Ibid.*, p. 332.

15. *Ibid.*, pp. 320, 333.

16. *Ibid.*, p. 300 f. Cf. Reuel L. Howe, *Man's Need and God's Action* (Greenwich: The Seabury Press, 1953), pp. 132 f., 135 f.; Harry Stack Sullivan, *The Interpersonal Theory of Psychiatry*, eds. Helen Swick Perry and Mary Ladd Gawel (New York: W. W. Norton & Co., 1953), pp. 204 f.

17. Bushnell, *op. cit.*, pp. 328 f.

18. *Ibid.*, p. 383.

19. *Ibid.*, p. 87.

20. *Ibid.*, pp. 252 f. Cf. Arnold Gesell, Frances L. Ilg, et al., *Child Development: An Introduction to the Study of Human Growth*, I, 360–63; cf. Yeaxlee, *op. cit.*, pp. 178–98; Dorothy W. Baruch, *Parents Can Be People: A Primer for and About Parents* (New York: Appleton-Century, 1944).

21. Cf. Gesell, Ilg, et al., *op. cit.*, II, 196 f.; Yeaxlee, *op. cit.*, pp. 88–118 (note especially p. 90).

chapter 4

1. George Stewart, *A History of Religious Education in Connecticut to the Middle of the Nineteenth Century*, eds. Luther A. Weigle and Henry B. Wright, "Yale Studies in the History and Theory of Religious Education" (New Haven: Yale University Press, 1924), I, 184 f.; Lewis Bevans Shenck, *The Presbyterian Doctrine of Children in the Covenant: An Historical Study of the Significance of Infant Baptism in the Presbyterian Church in America*, "Yale Studies in Religious Education" (New Haven: Yale University Press, 1940), XII, 55.

2. Sandford Fleming, *Children and Puritanism: The Place of Children in the Life and Thought of the New England Churches, 1620–1847*, "Yale Studies in Religious Education" (New Haven: Yale University Press, 1933), VIII, 39. He quotes from

Jonathan Edwards, *The Works of President Edwards in Four Volumes* (8th ed.; New York: Leavitt and Allen, 1852), IV, 317 f., 321.

3. Fleming, *op. cit.*, p. 166.

4. Barbara M. Cross, *Horace Bushnell: Minister to a Changing America* (Chicago: University of Chicago Press, 1958) is of valuable assistance in this respect.

chapter 5

1. Mary Bushnell Cheney, *Life and Letters of Horace Bushnell* (New York: Harper & Bros., 1880), p. 20.

2. Vol. X (1838).

3. Horace Bushnell, *Views of Christian Nurture and of Subjects Adjacent Thereto* (Hartford, Conn.: Edwin Hunt, 1847), p. 143.

4. Vol. II (1844).

5. Bushnell, *op. cit.*, p. 147.

6. *Ibid.*, p. 148.

7. *Ibid.* Italics added.

8. *Ibid.*, p. 153.

9. *Ibid.*, p. 161.

10. *Ibid.*, p. 168.

11. *Ibid.*, p. 178.

12. *Ibid.*, pp. 166 f.

13. Arthur Cushman McGiffert, *The Rise of Modern Religious Ideas* (New York: Macmillan, 1915), p. 277.

chapter 6

1. Horace Bushnell, *Christian Nurture* (New York: Charles Scribner's Sons, 1862), p. 10.

2. *Ibid.*, p. 108.

3. *Ibid.*, p. 31.

4. *Ibid.*, p. 100.

5. *Ibid.*, pp. 169 f.

6. *Ibid.*, p. 21. Italics added.

chapter 7

1. Horace Bushnell, *Christian Nurture* (New York: Charles Scribner's Sons, 1862), p. 17.

2. Horace Bushnell, *Nature and the Supernatural, as Together Constituting the One System of God* (New York: Charles Scribner's Sons, 1860).

3. Bushnell, *Christian Nurture*, op. cit., pp. 28 ff.

4. *Ibid.*, p. 16.

5. *Ibid.*, p. 68.

6. *Ibid.*, p. 192.

chapter 8

1. Horace Bushnell, *Views of Christian Nurture and of Subjects Adjacent Thereto* (Hartford, Conn.: Edwin Hunt, 1847), p. 51.

chapter 9

1. Horace Bushnell, *Views of Christian Nurture and of Subjects Adjacent Thereto* (Hartford, Conn.: Edwin Hunt, 1847), p. 4.

2. Theodore T. Munger, *Horace Bushnell: Preacher and Theologian* (Boston: Houghton Mifflin, 1899), p. 263.

3. Horace Bushnell, *God in Christ: Three Discourses Delivered at New Haven, Cambridge, and Andover, with a Preliminary Dissertation on Language* (centenary ed.; New York: Charles Scribner's Sons, 1910).

4. Horace Bushnell, *Christ in Theology: Being the Answer of the Author, Before the Hartford Central Association of Ministers, October, 1849, for the Doctrines of the Book Entitled "God in Christ"* (Hartford, Conn.: Brown and Parsons, 1851).

5. Munger, *op. cit.*, p. 156.

6. Barbara M. Cross, *Horace Bushnell: Minister to a Changing America* (Chicago: University of Chicago Press, 1958), pp. 94, 104, 107 f.

chapter 10

1. Horace Bushnell, *God in Christ: Three Discourses Delivered at New Haven, Cambridge, and Andover, with a Preliminary*

Dissertation on Language (centenary ed.; New York: Charles Scribner's Sons, 1910).

2. *Ibid.*, p. 122.

3. *Ibid.*, p. 137.

4. *Ibid.*, pp. 139 f.

5. *Ibid.*, p. 142.

6. *Ibid.*, p. 145.

7. *Ibid.*, p. 137; cf. pp. 173, 175 f.

8. Horace Bushnell, *Nature and the Supernatural, as Together Constituting the One System of God* (New York: Charles Scribner's Sons, 1860), pp. 36 f.

9. *Ibid.*, pp. 42 f., 86.

10. *Ibid.*, pp. 84 f.

11. *Ibid.*, p. 89.

12. *Ibid.*, p. 260.

13. *Ibid.*, p. 58.   Italics added.

14. *Ibid.*, p. 250.   Italics added.

15. *Ibid.*, pp. 171, 193, 342, 484.

16. *Ibid.*, pp. 493 f.

17. *Ibid.*, p. 276.

18. Horace Bushnell, *Christ in Theology: Being the Answer of the Author, Before the Hartford Central Association of Ministers, October, 1849, for the Doctrines of the Book Entitled "God in Christ"* (Hartford, Conn.: Brown and Parsons, 1851), p. 137.

19. Bushnell, *Nature and the Supernatural, op. cit.*, p. 101.

20. *Ibid.*, p. 408.   Italics added.

21. Horace Bushnell, *The Vicarious Sacrifice, Grounded in Principles Interpreted by Human Analogies* (New York: Charles Scribner's Sons, 1891), II, 235.

22. *Ibid.*, pp. 239 f.

chapter 11

1. Horace Bushnell, *Sermons on Living Subjects* (New York: Charles Scribner's Sons, 1887), p. 132.

2. Horace Bushnell, *God in Christ: Three Discourses Delivered at New Haven, Cambridge, and Andover, with a Preliminary Dissertation on Language* (centenary ed.; New York: Charles Scribner's Sons, 1910), p. 95.

3. Horace Bushnell, *Nature and the Supernatural, as Together Constituting the One System of God* (New York: Charles Scribner's Sons, 1860).

4. *Ibid.*, pp. 51, 58, 85.

5. *Ibid.*, p. 86.

6. *Ibid.*, pp. 54, 51 f.

7. *Ibid.*, pp. 96 f.

8. *Ibid.*, pp. 91–139.

9. *Ibid.*, pp. 103 f.

10. *Ibid.*, p. 110. Italics added.

11. *Ibid.*, p. 115.

12. *Ibid.*, p. 93.

13. *Ibid.*, p. 116.

14. Horace Bushnell, *Sermons for the New Life* (2d ed.; New York: Charles Scribner's Sons, 1858), p. 54.

15. Bushnell, *Sermons on Living Subjects, op. cit.*, p. 105.

16. Horace Bushnell, *The Spirit in Man: Sermons and Selections* (centenary ed.; New York: Charles Scribner's Sons, 1903), p. 40.

17. Bushnell, *Nature and the Supernatural, op. cit.*, p. 211.

18. *Ibid.*, p. 221.

19. *Ibid.*, p. 234.

20. *Ibid.*, pp. 223 f.

21. *Ibid.*, pp. 236, 374, 519.

22. *Ibid.*, p. 240.

23. *Ibid.*, p. 69.

24. Horace Bushnell, *Work and Play* (New York: Charles Scribner's Sons, 1883), pp. 78–123.

25. *Ibid.*, pp. 118 f.

26. *Ibid.*, pp. 122 f. Italics added.

chapter 12

1. Horace Bushnell, *God in Christ: Three Discourses Delivered at New Haven, Cambridge, and Andover, with a Preliminary Dissertation on Language* (centenary ed.; New York: Charles Scribner's Sons, 1910), pp. 119–81.

2. *Ibid.*, pp. 123–27.

3. *Ibid.*, p. 126.

4. *Ibid.*, p. 155.

5. *Ibid.*, p. 166.

6. *Ibid.*, p. 152.

7. *Ibid.*, p. 153.

8. *Ibid.*

9. Horace Bushnell, *Nature and the Supernatural, as Together Constituting the One System of God* (New York: Charles Scribner's Sons, 1860), pp. 276–332.

10. *Ibid.*, p. 293.

11. *Ibid.*

12. Bushnell, *God in Christ, op. cit.*, pp. 149 f.

13. Bushnell, *Nature and the Supernatural, op. cit.*, p. 240.

14. *Ibid.*, p. 276.

15. Bushnell, *God in Christ, op. cit.*, p. 191.

16. *Ibid.*, p. 195.

17. *Ibid.*, pp. 198–203.

18. *Ibid.*, p. 208.

19. *Ibid.*, pp. 208–11.

20. *Ibid.*, pp. 198, 207.

21. *Ibid.*, p. 216.

22. *Ibid.*

23. *Ibid.*, p. 215.

24. *Ibid.*, pp. 241 f.

25. Bushnell, *Nature and the Supernatural, op. cit.*, pp. 292, 296.

26. *Ibid.*, p. 297.

27. *Ibid.*, p. 296.

28. *Ibid.*, p. 322. Italics added.

29. Mary Bushnell Cheney, *Life and Letters of Horace Bushnell* (New York: Harper & Bros., 1880), pp. 478 f., 533, 541–44.

30. Horace Bushnell, *The Vicarious Sacrifice, Grounded in Principles Interpreted by Human Analogies,* Vol. II (New York: Charles Scribner's Sons, 1891).

31. Horace Bushnell, *Sermons on Living Subjects* (New York: Charles Scribner's Sons, 1887), p. 91.

32. Horace Bushnell, *Sermons for the New Life* (centenary ed.; New York: Charles Scribner's Sons, 1905), p. 128.

33. Horace Bushnell, *The Spirit in Man: Sermons and Selections* (centenary ed.; New York: Charles Scribner's Sons, 1903), pp. 41, 45.

34. Horace Bushnell, *Christ and His Salvation: In Sermons Variously Related Thereto* (3d ed.; New York: Charles Scribner's Sons, 1865), pp. 331, 420, 422.

chapter 13

1. Mary Bushnell Cheney, *Life and Letters of Horace Bushnell* (New York: Harper & Bros., 1880), p. 209.

2. Horace Bushnell, *God in Christ: Three Discourses Delivered at New Haven, Cambridge, and Andover, with a Preliminary Dissertation on Language* (centenary ed.; New York: Charles Scribner's Sons, 1910), p. 39.

3. *Ibid.*, p. 24.

4. *Ibid.*

5. *Ibid.*, p. 22.

6. *Ibid.*, p. 48; also pp. 44 f., 84.

7. *Ibid.*, p. 46. Italics added.

8. *Ibid.*, pp. 41 f., 48, 50, 52 f.

9. *Ibid.*, pp. 30 f.

10. *Ibid.*, p. 93.

11. *Ibid.*, pp. 95, 24.

12. Cheney, *op. cit.*, p. 208. Italics added.

13. Bushnell, *God in Christ, op. cit.*, pp. 12, 72, 77, 92.

14. *Ibid.*, pp. 56, 69 ff.

15. *Ibid.*, p. 73.

16. *Ibid.*, p. 96.

17. *Ibid.*, p. 315.

18. *Ibid.*, pp. 310–17.

19. Horace Bushnell, *Christian Nurture* (New York: Charles Scribner's Sons, 1862), p. 370.

chapter 14

1. Horace Bushnell, *God in Christ: Three Discourses Delivered at New Haven, Cambridge, and Andover, with a Preliminary Dissertation on Language* (centenary ed.; New York: Charles Scribner's Sons, 1910), p. 244.

2. Horace Bushnell, *Sermons on Living Subjects* (New York: Charles Scribner's Sons, 1887), p. 138.

3. *Ibid.* Italics added. Cf. Horace Bushnell, *Sermons for the New Life* (2d ed., New York: Charles Scribner's Sons, 1858), p. 108.

4. Horace Bushnell, *The Vicarious Sacrifice, Grounded in Principles Interpreted by Human Analogies* (New York: Charles Scribner's Sons, 1891), II, 403.

5. *Ibid.*, pp. 405, 404.

6. *Ibid.*, p. 404.

7. Bushnell, *Sermons for the New Life, op. cit.*, p. 124.

8. *Ibid.*, p. 94.

9. Bushnell, *Sermons on Living Subjects, op. cit.*, pp. 85 f.; cf. p. 119.

10. *Ibid.*, pp. 119 f.

11. Bushnell, *Sermons for the New Life, op. cit.*, p. 119.

12. Horace Bushnell, *Christ and His Salvation: In Sermons Variously Related Thereto* (3d ed.; New York: Charles Scribner's Sons, 1865), p. 440.

13. Bushnell, *Sermons for the New Life, op. cit.*, p. 116.

14. *Ibid.*, pp. 118 f.

15. *Ibid.*, pp. 119 f.

16. Bushnell, *Christ and His Salvation, op. cit.*, p. 303.

17. Bushnell, *Sermons for the New Life, op. cit.*, p. 115.

18. *Ibid.*, pp. 243–62.

19. *Ibid.*, pp. 247 f.

20. *Ibid.*, p. 249.

21. *Ibid.*, p. 247; cf. Horace Bushnell, *Views of Christian Nurture and of Subjects Adjacent Thereto* (Hartford, Conn.: Edwin Hunt, 1847), p. 15.

22. Bushnell, *Sermons on Living Subjects, op. cit.*, p. 229; cf. pp. 303 f.

23. *Ibid.*, p. 300.

24. Bushnell, *The Vicarious Sacrifice, op. cit.*, I, 524–37.

chapter 15

1. Horace Bushnell, *God in Christ: Three Discourses Delivered at New Haven, Cambridge, and Andover, with a Preliminary Dissertation on Language* (centenary ed.; New York: Charles Scribner's Sons, 1910).

2. A. J. William Myers, *Horace Bushnell and Religious Education* (Boston: Manthorne and Burack, Inc., 1937), pp. 162 f. Myers quotes the words of Dr. Thomas from *The Congregationalist and Christian World*, LXXXVII, No. 23 (June, 1902), 812 f.; cf. Reuen Thomas, *Leaders of Thought in Modern Church* (Boston: D. Lothrop Co., 1892), p. 148.

3. H. H. Goodwin, "Horace Bushnell," *The New Englander*, XXXIX (1880), 803–27; XL or new series IV (1881), 1–39.

4. VI (1886), 113–30.

5. Myers, *op. cit.*, pp. 148–77.

6. *Ibid.*, pp. 156, 167.

7. *Ibid.*, pp. 156 f.; Frank Hugh Foster, *The Modern Movement in American Theology: Sketches in the History of American Protestant Thought from the Civil War to the World War* (New York: Fleming H. Revell Co., 1939), p. 20.

8. Washington Gladden, *Recollections* (Boston: Houghton Mifflin, 1909), p. 167.

9. Theodore T. Munger, *Horace Bushnell: Preacher and Theologian* (Boston: Houghton Mifflin, 1899), pp. 95 f.; also p. 413.

10. Williston Walker, "Dr. Bushnell as a Religious Leader," *Bushnell Centenary: Minutes of the General Association of Connecticut at the One Hundred and Ninety-Third Annual Meeting Held in Hartford, June 17, 18, 1902* (Hartford, Conn.: The Case, Lockwood and Brainard Co., 1902), p. 34.

11. John Wright Buckham, *Progressive Religious Thought in America: A Survey of the Enlarging Pilgrim Faith* (Boston: Houghton Mifflin, 1919), p. 29.

12. *Ibid.*, pp. 6 f.

13. Foster, *op. cit.*, pp. 59 f. Italics added.

14. Walter Marshall Horton, *Realistic Theology* (New York: Harper & Bros., 1934), p. 26. Italics added.

15. *Ibid.*, p. 30.

16. George Hammar, *Christian Realism in Contemporary American Theology: A Study of Reinhold Niebuhr, W. M. Horton, and H. P. Van Dusen, Preceded by a General and Historical Survey* (Upsala, Sweden: A. B. Lundequistaka Bokhandeln, 1940).

17. H. Richard Niebuhr, *The Kingdom of God in America* (Chicago: Willet, Clark and Co., 1937), p. 193.

18. *Ibid.*

19. *Ibid.*, p. 194.

20. Edward Clinton Gardner, "Man as Sinner in Nineteenth Century New England Theology: A Study in the Challenge of Romantic Humanitarianism" (unpublished Ph.D. dissertation, Yale University, 1952); cf. E. Clinton Gardner, "Horace Bushnell's Concept of Responses: A Fresh Approach to the Doctrine of Ability and Inability," *Religion in Life: A Christian Quarterly of Opinion and Discussion,* XXVII (1957–58), 119–31.

chapter 16

1. A. J. William Myers, *Horace Bushnell and Religious Education* (Boston: Manthorne and Burack, Inc., 1937), p. 104.

2. Harrison S. Elliott, *Can Religious Education Be Christian?* (New York: Macmillan, 1940), p. 31; cf. p. 33.

3. H. Clay Trumbull, *My Four Religious Teachers: Charles G. Finney, David Hawley, Elias R. Beadle, Horace Bushnell* (Philadelphia: The Sunday School Times Co., 1903), pp. 10 f.

4. *Ibid.*, pp. 104 f., 108.

5. Elliott, *op. cit.*, p. 25.

6. Francis E. Clark, *The Children and the Church, and the Young People's Society of Christian Endeavor, as a Means of Bringing Them Together* (3d ed., revised and enlarged; Boston: Congregational Sunday School and Publishing Society, 1882), p. 12; cf. p. 22.

7. Mary Bushnell Cheney, *Life and Letters of Horace Bushnell* (New York: Harper & Bros., 1880), pp. 224, 228, 571.

8. Amos B. Chesebrough, *Children Trained for Discipleship: Arguments and Suggestions for the Consideration of Pastors and Christian Parents and Teachers* (New York: Anson D. P. Randolph and Co., 1883).

9. *Ibid.*, pp. 7, 27, 41, 29, 44–66.

10. Adelaide Teague Case, "Christian Education," *The Church Through Half a Century: Essays in Honor of William Adams Brown by Former Students*, eds., Samuel McCrea Cavert and Henry Pitney Van Dusen (New York: Charles Scribner's Sons, 1936), pp. 230 ff.

11. *The Religious Education Association: Proceedings of the First Annual Convention, Chicago, February 10–12, 1903* (Chicago: Executive Office of the Association, 1903), p. 45. Italics added.

12. *Ibid.*, p. 46.

13. *Ibid.*, p. 52.

14. Horace Bushnell, *Christian Nurture* (New York: Charles Scribner's Sons, 1862), p. 22.

15. George Albert Coe, *What Is Christian Education?* (New York: Charles Scribner's Sons, 1929), p. 296.

16. William C. Bower, *The Curriculum of Religious Education* (New York: Charles Scribner's Sons, 1925), p. 259.

17. Myers, *op. cit.*, pp. 104, 115, 123, 131; Elliott, *op. cit.*, pp. 31 f., 45 f., 228.

18. Edward Payson Hammond, *The Conversion of Children* (Chicago: Fleming H. Revell Co., 1917).

19. Luther A. Weigle, *The Pupil and the Teacher* (New York: George H. Doran Co., 1911), p. 195.

20. Luther A. Weigle, "Christian Religious Education," *The Jerusalem Meeting of the International Missionary Council, March 24–April 8, 1929* (New York: International Missionary Council, 1928), II, 179 f.

21. Luther A. Weigle, *Jesus and the Educational Method* (Nashville: Abingdon Press, 1939).

22. *Christian Education Today: A Statement of Basic Philosophy.* Approved February, 1940, by the Educational Commission (Chicago: The International Council of Religious Education, 1940), p. 16.

23. Horace Bushnell, *Christian Nurture*; introd. by Luther A. Weigle (New Haven: Yale University Press, 1947).

24. Paul Vieth, ed., *The Church and Christian Education* (St. Louis: Bethany Press, 1947).

25. James D. Smart, *The Teaching Ministry of the Church: An Examination of the Basic Principles of Christian Education* (Philadelphia: Westminster Press, 1954), p. 67.